Additional Books for Parents of Preteens and Teens From the American Academy of Pediatrics

healthychildren.org
Powered by pediatricians. Trusted by parents.
from the American Academy of Pediatrics

For additional parenting resources, visit the He
https://shop.aap.org/for-p

T0002227

You·ology

A PUBERTY GUIDE
FOR EVERY BODY

MELISA HOLMES, MD, FACOG | **TRISH HUTCHISON**, MD, FAAP
KATHRYN LOWE, MD, FAAP

American Academy of Pediatrics
DEDICATED TO THE HEALTH OF ALL CHILDREN®

American Academy of Pediatrics Publishing Staff
Mary Lou White, *Chief Product and Services Officer/SVP, Membership, Marketing, and Publishing*
Mark Grimes, *Vice President, Publishing*
Kathryn Sparks, *Senior Editor, Consumer Publishing*
Shannan Martin, *Production Manager, Consumer Publications*
Amanda Helmholz, *Medical Copy Editor*
Sara Hoerdeman, *Marketing Manager, Consumer Products*

Published by the American Academy of Pediatrics
345 Park Blvd
Itasca, IL 60143
Telephone: 630/626-6000
Facsimile: 847/434-8000
www.aap.org

The American Academy of Pediatrics is an organization of 67,000 primary care pediatricians, pediatric medical subspecialists, and pediatric surgical specialists dedicated to the health, safety, and well-being of all infants, children, adolescents, and young adults.

The information contained in this publication should not be used as a substitute for the medical care and advice of your pediatrician. There may be variations in treatment that your pediatrician may recommend based on individual facts and circumstances.

Statements and opinions expressed are those of the authors and not necessarily those of the American Academy of Pediatrics.

Any websites, brand names, products, or manufacturers are mentioned for informational and identification purposes only and do not imply an endorsement by the American Academy of Pediatrics (AAP). The AAP is not responsible for the content of external resources. Information was current at the time of publication.

This publication has been developed by the American Academy of Pediatrics. The contributors are expert authorities in the field of pediatrics. No commercial involvement of any kind has been solicited or accepted in the development of the content of this publication. Disclosures: Melisa Holmes and Trish Hutchison have a relationship with Girlology, Inc. Kathryn Lowe reports no conflicts of interest.

Every effort is made to keep *You-ology: A Puberty Guide for EVERY Body* consistent with the most recent advice and information available from the American Academy of Pediatrics.

Special discounts are available for bulk purchases of this publication. Email Special Sales at nationalaccounts@aap.org for more information.

Printed in the United States of America

9-470/0222   3 4 5 6 7 8 9 10
CB0127
ISBN: 978-1-61002-569-0
eBook: 978-1-61002-572-0
EPUB: 978-1-61002-570-6

Cover and publication design by Scott Rattray Design
Illustrations by Lisa Perrett

Library of Congress Control Number: 2021904858

As a mom of a transgender daughter, I'm delighted that *You-ology* explains and illustrates puberty in an inclusive and sensitive manner. Knowledge is key to acceptance and this groundbreaking guide recognizes, in a clear and understandable narrative, that puberty can be certain and sometimes unique for every youth.

> Jeanette Jennings, president and cofounder of the TransKids Purple Rainbow Foundation, mom of trans youth activist Jazz Jennings, and cast member of the award-winning TLC docuseries, *I Am Jazz*

Since humans existed, bodies have developed in fairly predictable ways…so why is talking to our kids about puberty *still* so hard? If "the puberty talk" were simply about anatomy, it would be an easy conversation to have—or pamphlet to hand over. But your child's changing body elicits so many new feelings and reactions (from them and other people), growing up gets complicated, quickly. *You-ology* expertly helps kids and parents through the physical, social, and emotional aspects of entering adolescence, from being teased for how your body is or isn't developing to what things you can say when someone crosses your boundaries. This is the guide every parent and child needs to develop a comfortable and confident acceptance of their own bodies and others!

> Michelle Icard, author of *Fourteen Talks by Age Fourteen*

You-ology is the much-needed book about puberty that covers not just the physical but also the emotional changes that youth go through in a gender-inclusive way that normalizes everyone's puberty experience. While most parents won't have a gender-diverse child, most, if not all, youth will have peers who are gender diverse. Using an ethnically and gender-diverse cast of characters and inclusive terminology such as *bodies with ovaries* and *bodies with testes,* every body's experience is outlined in *You-ology,* allowing every youth to be able to see themselves while understanding their peers' experiences and know that they can be comfortable exactly as they are.

> Paria Hassouri, MD, FAAP, author of *Found in Transition: A Mother's Evolution During Her Child's Gender Change* and director of the Pediatric and Adolescent Gender Wellness Clinic at Cedars-Sinai Medical Center, Los Angeles, CA

You-ology is honest, accepting, empowering, and medically accurate. It reads like a personalized how-to-do-puberty book for kids. Readers will know "they got this" when it comes to managing the amazing changes caused by puberty.

> Damon Korb, MD, FAAP, author of *Raising an Organized Child: 5 Steps to Boost Independence, Ease Frustration, and Promote Confidence* and director, Center for Developing Minds, Los Gatos, CA

This is the book about puberty that kids and parents deserve! Not only is it medically accurate, but it is also free of shame and covers topics like gender diversity in thorough, thoughtful detail. My kids will be reading this for sure!

> Jennifer Lincoln, MD, IBCLC, author of *Let's Talk About Down There: An OB-GYN Answers All Your Burning Questions…Without Making You Feel Embarrassed for Asking* and board-certified obstetrician-gynecologist practicing in Portland, OR

Sex education…the class EVERYBODY hates. Now young people have a book that not only responds to that youthful lament but gives them the gift of a gender-inclusive body-positive explanation of puberty. *You-ology* is that gift and a wonderful addition to youths', parents', and educators' book collections as children make their way through the puberty journey.

> Diane Ehrensaft, PhD, author of *Gender Born, Gender Made* and *The Gender Creative Child;* director of mental health, Child and Adolescent Gender Center at the University of California San Francisco (UCSF) Benioff Children's Hospital; and associate professor of pediatrics, UCSF

Puberty can be awkward for all kids, but for those whose bodies are a little different—due to disability, medical conditions, or gender identity—it can be excruciating. *You-ology* is a book where kids can see their bodies and their uniqueness reflected back at them. This book is about real kids going through real changes. It discusses issues such as changing social relationships, social media, bullying, and crushes in a way that is normalizing (eg, it's OK to have crushes…or not) and reflects adolescents' current experiences rather than relying on adults' outdated assumptions of what puberty looks like. And best of all, it's funny. It embraces the humor of having a body that sometimes does unexpected things and the awkwardness of having to talk about them.

I wish this book had been around when I was a kid, and I will definitely be recommending it to my patients, my friends, and my own kids.

> Ilana Sherer, MD, pediatrician; executive committee, American Academy of Pediatrics Section on LGBT Health and Wellness; and cofounder, Child and Adolescent Gender Center at the UCSF Benioff Children's Hospital

Honest, relatable, informative, and inclusive. I hope every kid gets to read this to learn about puberty.

> Juanita Hodax, MD, FAAP, pediatric endocrinologist and codirector of the Seattle Children's Gender Clinic

You-ology is the puberty book that we pediatricians have been waiting for! With inclusion at the center and a cast of relatable characters sharing their stories, this is the perfect book for tweens and families starting their own puberty journeys.

> Hina Talib, MD, pediatrician and adolescent medicine specialist at Atria Institute and associate professor of pediatrics at Children's Hospital at Montefiore

Finally, a comprehensive guide that combines a high degree of gender literacy with medically sound concepts and approaches that speak to ALL young people.

> Joel Baum, MS, senior director for professional development, Gender Spectrum, San Leandro, CA

Finally, a comprehensive puberty book for EVERY body! This will be my go-to recommendation for kids and their families.

> Maggie Zamboni, MD, FAAP

You-ology is a refreshing, honest, funny, positive, and medically accurate puberty guide for every child. What a gift to have one book to help guide all of my patients through puberty! You can read this book with your kids and giggle or let them read this in private and talk about it.

> Dawn Kallio, MD, FAAP

Inclusive and affirming, *You-ology* is a must-read puberty guide for both parents and kids. This fun and engaging book covers the most important topics and answers the questions I get asked most as a practitioner. Following the personal stories of each unique character makes it so anyone who reads this book has an experience they can identify with—a puberty book for everyone!

Katherine Mistretta, DNP, APRN, FNP-BC, WPATH GEI SOC7

Creatively written and beautifully illustrated, *You-ology: A Puberty Guide for EVERY Body* offers an inclusive and friendly format for young people to access engaging short stories and answer clearly their questions about their changing bodies. Teachers, parents, and caregivers will all appreciate the intentional ways in which the authors curated for their readers a text experience like this!

Morgan L. Darby, MA, MAT, director of equity and inclusion, The Children's School, Atlanta, GA; former education program director, Gender Spectrum, San Leandro, CA; and founding board member, Harbor Camps

For EVERY person approaching puberty, in puberty, or trying to figure out what just happened in puberty. We see you.

Equity, Diversity, and Inclusion Statement

The American Academy of Pediatrics is committed to principles of equity, diversity, and inclusion in its publishing program. Editorial boards, author selections, and author transitions (publication succession plans) are designed to include diverse voices that reflect society as a whole. Editor and author teams are encouraged to actively seek out diverse authors and reviewers at all stages of the editorial process. Publishing staff are committed to promoting equity, diversity, and inclusion in all aspects of publication writing, review, and production.

CONTENTS

A MESSAGE TO PARENTS

Dear Parents,

Do you remember your own puberty education (if you got it at all)? For many of us, it was brief, awkward, and segregated by gender. Our children deserve something better—that's why we wrote *You-ology*. It's honest, cringe-free, and for EVERY body.

For nearly 2 decades, we've led puberty education programs across the country for thousands of children, and as physicians, we've gathered countless experiences from young people to inform this book and best support you.

In this book, we provide medically accurate, age-appropriate information about how puberty works for EVERY body. We feature short stories from everyday kids to normalize common challenges. We explain the physical and emotional changes of puberty in kid-friendly language. Everyone will learn about erections and sperm. Everyone will learn about periods. Everyone will get hygiene tips. And we explain puberty for gender-diverse kids because even if you haven't personally experienced gender diversity in your own family, your child is certain to have a friend or classmate who is gender diverse.

How can this book help your child?

- Your child will gain confidence and experience less anxiety over what's happening to their body—or what's ahead. Our short stories normalize common challenges, and we answer your child's questions in a simple and medically accurate way. Most of all, they'll know that their own experiences and feelings are normal!

- Every child is wonderfully curious and loves learning how the body works and grows. We explain the physical and emotional changes of puberty in kid-friendly language. That means boys, girls, and gender-diverse kids can all understand each other better. This understanding helps grow respect for all, which creates a better world for everyone.

- When children understand what their peers experience, they grow up more empathetic and supportive. As parents, we all want our kids to grow up this way, and that's why this book is inclusive.

We hope you're eager to help the children you care about prepare for their own puberty and understand puberty for EVERY body.

With gratitude and support for all kids,

Melisa Holmes, MD
Trish Hutchison, MD
Kathryn Lowe, MD

MEET THE CHARACTERS

You-ology is not just full of facts. There are stories that start off each chapter. In the stories, you'll meet a group of kids who go to the same school and who are all in the age range when most kids go through puberty. There are 6 main characters, and plenty of other characters show up throughout the stories as well. You might see some similarities to you and your friends as you read about the challenging situations they face and the ways they manage them as they learn about themselves and each other.

Here's a bit of information about the main characters.

Maria has super short hair, is very athletic, and doesn't like makeup or jewelry. She loves racing remote control cars! In school, she struggles with reading, but she's great at math and loves to draw. She wants to be an architect and an athlete.

Hey, I'm Maria! It's my dream to become a famous soccer player.

Jack likes to listen to all types of music. He plays guitar and wants to learn how to play piano and drums, and one day, he wants to start a band! His mom is the biggest baseball fan he knows, and he loves watching games with her while they're sharing popcorn.

Hi, my name is Jack! I play guitar in the school band.

Hey! I'm Kimi. I play drums and love musical theater!

Kimi's favorite activities are singing, dancing, and making music. She loves going to the beach with her family and swimming all day. One day, she wants to learn how to surf! Kimi is proud to be transgender, but she is waiting to share that information with her friends when she feels ready.

Nice to meet you! I'm Leshaun. I like to hang out with my friends at the pool, and one day, I want to be an actor!

Leshaun is a boy who loves to wear his purple skinny jeans, is terrified of spiders, and has a big-time crush on Stephanie. He wants to be an actor and go away to an acting summer camp, but he gets homesick when he's away from his family.

I'm Oliver! I read a lot of comics and love playing board games with my older brother.

Oliver not only loves to cosplay (dressing up as his favorite comic book and movie characters) but also loves to ride dirt bikes. His best friend is Jazmin, and they like to play basketball and foosball. He really likes hanging out with his older brother, David.

Stephanie loves anything frilly and fancy, and she's the captain of her school's robotics team. She has been coding since she was 5 years old and loves computers as much as glitter (and her new puppy, Champ!). Her older sister has Down syndrome. Stephanie always goes to her first when she needs advice. They have fun giving each other makeovers.

I'm Stephanie! I take all kinds of dance classes, and I like to code. Also, this is my new puppy, Champ!

Here are some other characters you will meet!

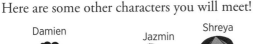

CHAPTER 1

PUBERTY: HERE'S THE DEAL

The gymnasium echoes with noise as the students of Bright Springs School fill up row after row of empty seats. Today is Guest Speaker Day, which takes place every year during the first week of school, and everyone is excited to see who the mysterious speaker will be. Last year, the author of an adventure book series came to speak about writing. The year before, a zoologist explained his job studying and caring for animals, and he even brought a live snake that some of the kids got to hold!

Oliver remembers what his older brother, David, said about his favorite Guest Speaker Day: a famous band came and gave a live concert after their speeches, and David and his friends got interviewed on the radio.

Maria and Stephanie grab seats next to each other in the front row. They've heard a rumor that the guest speaker is some kind of famous athlete, and Maria wants to be close just in case the speaker is one of her favorite soccer players.

"Quiet down, everyone," Principal Ahmad says from the stage, tapping the microphone with his finger. Slowly, the gymnasium settles down, with even the excited chatter settling into silence. "I'm honored to be introducing this year's Guest Speaker Day presenter. I think it's going to be the best one yet!"

The students erupt in applause before settling down again.

"I think it's going to be the president," Jack whispers to his friend Leshaun.

"Um, I think the president has more important things to be doing," Leshaun whispers back.

"It's the vice president, at least," Jack whispers.

Principal Ahmad clears his throat, and the room gets quiet.

"Without further ado," the principal says, "please give a warm welcome to Dr Sarah Wilson, who is here to talk with you about the important, exciting, universal topic of . . . *puberty*!"

The room is silent. Then there is an awkward, scattered applause as a woman walks onto the stage.

"*Puberty*?!" Kimi exclaims. She thought Guest Speaker Day was supposed to be *fun.* All around her, her friends echo her disbelief.

"Yes!" Stephanie exclaims, grabbing onto Maria's hand in excitement. "This is way better than an athlete!"

"It is?" Maria asks.

"Yes!" Stephanie squeezes Maria's hand. "We're going to be adults!"

"Right now?" Maria replies, sounding nervous.

On the other side of the gym, Leshaun looks over at Jack.

"You know, I'm actually kind of curious about this," he says. "I want to know more about that period thing."

"I already know all this stuff," Jack whispers back.

"Maybe you think you do," Leshaun says, "but you don't."

I wish I had called in sick, Oliver thinks, knowing many other kids are probably thinking the same.

Dr Wilson takes the stage and waits for the whispers to stop.

"Hello, everyone," she says, with her voice echoing into the microphone. "I'm so happy to be here today to speak with you about puberty."

She smiles at the crowd. "*Everyone* goes through puberty. It's normal to be a little nervous about it. But it's also normal to be excited! You're all growing up, and that means new changes and choices."

Someone in the back of the room raises their hand.

"Yes?" Dr Wilson asks, pointing to the back of the gym. "Do we have a question?"

Across the gymnasium, heads turn, but no one can see whom she called on.

"Um," the voice says, "what's *puberty*?"

Growing up? Really? Did an adult just give you this book? Did you roll your eyes or did you laugh a little? Either reaction would be normal because this book is going to give you a lot of information that may seem awkward. It can also be a little funny, but it's really important. It's about puberty—that time when your body starts changing to look more grown up.

Puberty is a pretty unusual word. What exactly does it mean? Well, the word *puberty* comes from Latin words that mean "adulthood" and "to grow hairy or mossy." Yep, hairy. That's pretty descriptive, isn't it?

To say it simply, puberty is the time when your body changes from being childlike to being more adultlike. For most people, it takes about 5 years to get all the way through puberty. It takes a long time to make a masterpiece!

Most girls and kids like Oliver start puberty between the ages of 8 and 13 years. Most boys and kids like Kimi start between 9 and 14. Many of the changes are the same for EVERY body (like growing taller and having new body odors), but some of the changes are different depending on your body parts (we bet you knew that already). So, remember, sometimes it may seem as if you are the only one dealing with body changes, but EVERY body goes through puberty.

WHY PUBERTY?

It's no secret that your body has to go through these changes so one day you can help make a baby if you choose to. That's how the human species continues. Going through puberty is also just part of becoming an adult, being able to do the important things adults do, and growing into the best version of you. These changes mean your body will grow bigger and your private parts will get an extreme makeover.

EVERY body goes through puberty, but not everyone gets the chance to learn how and why it happens. As doctors, we wanted to write this book because we know that kids are curious—not only about their own bodies but also about their friends' bodies. We also know that when you understand what's happening to your body, you worry less and you better care for yourself. So whether you're learning about your own body or about bodies that are different from yours, it's normal to be curious, and it's great to understand that puberty is for EVERY body.

Learning about this stuff might make you feel excited, interested, embarrassed, or just plain awkward. However you're feeling is normal. Keep reading. The more you learn, the more comfortable you'll be.

WHAT ARE HORMONES?

Puberty actually starts in the brain, so you can't see or feel the very beginning. It all begins when the brain sends out these things called **hormones.**

Have you ever heard someone mention hormones? Sometimes, hormones are blamed for stuff like cranky moods or silly behavior, but hormones are actually helpful. Hormones act as chemical messengers that tell your body parts important things, like when to go to sleep or when to grow. Hormones also control your energy. They tell you when you're hungry and even how much pee to make. Guess what else they control? Yep, puberty.

During puberty, there are hormones that tell your body to grow faster, hormones that tell your breasts or **testes**

FUN FACT:

Humans aren't the only group that goes through puberty. Lots of animals also go through puberty as they grow into their adult look. They may not break out in zits, but many change body shapes, grow new colors, and show new attitudes.

(TEST eez) (also known as **testicles,** or maybe you know them as "balls") to start growing, hormones that tell your hair to sprout in new places, and hormones that cause new smells to creep out of your armpits.

WHEN WILL THESE CHANGES HAPPEN?

We bet you're wondering exactly when these changes will start or stop. The actual moment when your brain says "GO!" is sort of a mystery. Scientists still haven't figured out exactly what makes it happen, so there's no answer that works for EVERY body.

Just as you are unique in the things you like to do, the sound of your laugh, and the foods you like to eat for breakfast, the way your body looks is also totally unique. That means it will follow its own schedule—yours and yours alone. And your best friend will have *their* own schedule. And the person who sits next to you in math class will have *their* own schedule too.

You have to remember that being different is normal, even when it doesn't feel that way. It's actually really neat the way everyone goes through puberty changes, but each person goes through these on their own schedule and gets their own look at the end.

WHAT'S HAPPENING?

Growing Bigger

Growing is one of the first signs of puberty. A hormone called **growth hormone** (that's easy to remember) increases a ton during puberty to make you grow fast. But you won't go to bed as a kid and wake up as a full-grown adult. Growth hormone changes your body size over a long time, and it starts somewhere you might not expect.

Actually, before all the private stuff starts happening, your hands and feet start to grow! So when you find yourself outgrowing your sneakers faster than normal, you can smile to yourself and know puberty is starting!

You probably already know that the fun doesn't end there. There are other hormones called **estrogen** (ES tra jin) and **testosterone** (tes TOS ter own) that cause most of the changes to your private parts. A tiny, pea-sized gland in the brain, called the **pituitary** (puh TU uh tary) **gland,** sends a chemical messenger (yep, another hormone) to the testes or **ovaries** to tell them to start making hormones.

Testes make a lot of testosterone.

Ovaries make a lot of estrogen and a little testosterone.

Throughout this book, we tell you more about what each of these hormones does.

Growing Smarter Too

Remember how puberty all started in your brain? Well, as your brain starts sending out the messenger hormones, it starts going through some changes of its own. That means your brain is growing smarter and getting ready to learn totally new things. Cool!

Around the age of 11, your brain can start to understand things that didn't make sense when you were younger. For example, your brain can start to understand things you can't necessarily see, like justice and beliefs.

Your brain can also begin to understand more complicated things, like algebra. Ask your teachers! They know that it's pretty difficult to teach even simple algebra to a first grader, but by middle school, most kids "get it."

All these brain changes also mean that you can think about things that happened in the past and learn from them. Then you can take what you learned and use it to make better decisions.

For example, let's say a new friend you'd been wanting to hang out with invited you over after school. In your excitement, you ran home, changed clothes, and went to their house without doing your homework. You had such a great time that your friend's mom invited you to stay for dinner, and by the time you went back home, it was time to get ready for bed. You never did your homework, so you received a zero in 2 classes and a low grade on the vocabulary quiz you should have studied for. You were then grounded for 2 weeks! The next time you were invited to your friend's house, you remembered what happened last time. So, instead of rushing over, you took your time to do your homework first, so you wouldn't receive zeros and end up grounded again. Instead of making the same mistake, your brain kicked in and said, "Hold on! Remember what happened last time?! If you let that happen again, you'll miss a lot of fun!"

When you were 6, that conversation in your head probably wouldn't have happened. Now that you are starting to think more maturely, you can make better decisions. And making good decisions is what helps you stay smart and safe. For now, this part about thinking better may sound a little confusing, but it will make more sense as your brain grows in puberty.

FUN FACT:

The adult human brain weighs about 3 pounds and is 2% of the entire body weight. It can store about *2.5 million gigabytes* of digital memory (one type of smartphone today holds up to only 512 gigabytes). The sperm whale has the biggest animal brain, and it can weigh up to 20 pounds. Don't you wonder how much information it can hold?

FEELING WEIRD?

Because puberty is a time of so many changes, it is perfectly natural for you to feel a little weird or worried about all that's going on. You might feel more **modest.** That means you want privacy when you dress and undress, or you want to keep your naked body private. Sometimes, you might even feel embarrassed about your changing body parts. It's also normal to be curious about how your friends' bodies are changing. You might wonder whether your changes are like theirs.

The most important thing to remember is that all the changes happen a little differently for everyone. So if your changes are not exactly like your friends', don't worry. Most kids feel at least a little worried or weird at some point during this whole puberty thing.

Just remember, your body is doing exactly what it's supposed to do, on its own schedule. If you see growing up as something positive (which it really is), you'll get through it feeling happier and more excited about all the amazing things your body is doing. Growing up can feel a little strange, but there are a lot of great things about it.

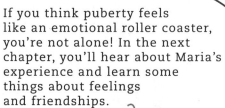

If you think puberty feels like an emotional roller coaster, you're not alone! In the next chapter, you'll hear about Maria's experience and learn some things about feelings and friendships.

CHAPTER 2

FEELINGS AND FRIENDS

MARIA

I walk into the cafeteria, feeling like I could fly and enjoying the way my hair no longer bounces against my shoulders. My new, very short haircut makes me look like my favorite professional soccer player or like my mom's favorite actress—no more hair getting in my way while I'm playing sports or taking a test! It feels *amazing*.

"There goes the new boy again," Shreya announces as I walk by her table. The girls around her laugh and cover their mouths. One of them even snorts.

My skin goes hot, and my hands clench into tight fists at my sides. But I force myself to take a deep breath and keep walking past their table. Shreya has been making fun of my haircut all day, and her jabs make me feel a little worse every time. I don't even understand what's going on. Why does she care what my hair looks like?

"Don't listen to her," Jazmin says when I sit down next to her. "You look amazing."

"Yeah," adds Stephanie, "Shreya's just jealous."

I shrug, feeling the redness slowly fade from my face. "It's no big deal," I say. But I think my appetite got up and ran out of the cafeteria as soon as Shreya had opened her mouth.

Stephanie and Jazmin start talking about the latest episode of our favorite TV show. Jazmin distracts me with homemade sugar cookies, and I laugh at stories of Stephanie's new puppy, forgetting all about Shreya's comments. Today has been an emotional roller coaster, but I'm finally back on a high peak, flying downhill with a smile on my face.

Before I know it, I'm in art class, my favorite place at school. Ms Chen has the most incredible collection of paints, which mix together into every shade I can imagine. I'm in the middle of mixing red, white, and yellow into the perfect peachy pink when I hear a giggle from the table next to mine.

"Shreya," Damien whispers, "did you have an accident?"

More laughs from the table. I look over and see Shreya notice the brown paint she's gotten all over her pants. Her cheeks flush pink, and her eyes start to shine with tears. Then she stands up and hurries out of the classroom.

"I'm sorry! It was just a joke!" Damien calls after her, actually looking sorry. But Shreya is already gone.

I set down my paintbrush and take a deep breath. Then I stand up and follow Shreya into the hall.

"What do you want?!" Shreya snaps when I arrive. She sniffles and wipes a tear from her cheek.

"To make sure you are OK," I say. "I know how it hurts to be made fun of."

Shreya blinks at me through watery eyes.

"I'm sorry," she says, "I've been so mean to you today. I don't even know why I did it. But I'm really sorry if I made you feel anything like this."

"You did," I tell her. "It's OK. I hope you'll remember how this feels and won't do it again."

Shreya wipes the last of the tears from her eyes and nods. "I won't." She sniffles again. "Thanks for coming out here with me. That was really cool."

I nod and then give her a small smile. "Now let's get back inside. I think Damien wants to apologize to you too."

So now you know that puberty changes more than the way you look. It also changes your brain, which controls the way you think and feel. And guess what? The way you think may change some of your interests. The way you feel can change the way you act. Finally, all of these together can change some of your friendships and the way you act around other people. That means puberty is not just about bodies changing but about feelings and friendships changing too!

IS IT HORMONES?

We know that a lot of grown-ups think young people's moods and attitudes are all caused by hormones, but actually, your moods come from your brain. As puberty begins, your changing brain and your new hormones make you feel emotions bigger and faster than ever before. Bigger feelings and emotions happen to everyone. When everyone is dealing with these, it can definitely affect friendships. You may feel happy and giggly one minute, then something suddenly makes you sad or tearful. It's OK. Big feelings can be confusing and hard to manage, but they're normal. It takes practice to learn how to handle them in ways that are healthy.

In this chapter, we talk about managing your bigger emotions and why it's important to learn how. Most of all, we want you to learn to be true to yourself and respectful to everyone. With new moods and attitudes, sometimes they're easy and fun. Sometimes they're a real challenge!

FUN FACT:

Laughter really is the best medicine. When you laugh, your body releases hormones that make you feel better and keep you healthier. And kids are best at it! Adults laugh about only 15 to 100 times a day, but 6-year-olds laugh about 3 times more than adults. It's good for you!

EASY AND DIFFICULT EMOTIONS

Where do emotions come from anyway? They don't just show up without any reason. Your brain notices everything that happens to you, and it sends out emotions to help you pay attention. Everyone experiences a lot of different emotions over time—even within one day. When good things are happening, you may

notice emotions that are easy to feel, like happiness, excitement, or love. But when you experience things that are scary or hurtful, you will notice emotions that are more difficult for you, like fear, anger, loneliness, or disappointment.

Did you notice we said *easy* and *difficult*, NOT good and bad? That's because there are no bad or wrong emotions. All emotions are important—even the difficult ones. It's just harder to manage our difficult emotions.

When You Struggle

"Name It to Tame It"

Have you ever noticed that when you let out or show your difficult emotions, people around you say something like "Calm down," "Don't cry," or "Don't be sad"? People who say that might be trying to help, but it's not always great advice. You can't stop your emotions, and hiding them inside makes you feel worse. Letting them out in a healthy way is a lot better for you.

How do you do that? The first step is to think about how you're feeling and name your emotion. Are you sad? Frustrated? Disappointed? Jealous? Worried? The following box lists lots of words you can use to describe how you're feeling. A big emotion can feel like a wild animal roaring in your body. Once you name it, you'll have an easier time taming it, which means you'll move it out of your brain and body. The way you handle or manage emotions is called your *coping skills.* There are lots of healthy ways to manage your emotions. Keep reading!

afraid	delighted	happy	satisfied
angry	disappointed	hurt	scared
annoyed	discouraged	irritated	shy
anxious	disgusted	jealous	silly
ashamed	embarrassed	lonely	sorry
awful	excited	loved	terrific
bored	fragile	mad	thankful
calm	frustrated	mean	tickled
cheerful	furious	miserable	uncomfortable
confident	glad	moody	unhappy
confused	gloomy	proud	vulnerable
content	grumpy	relaxed	worried

Be Cool

Many of our difficult emotions can make us feel angry. What helps you cool off when you are really angry? Sometimes you may become so angry, you want to break something or hurt someone, but you probably know that those are never the right choices. Instead, think of some things you can do when you are angry so nobody is hurt and nothing is broken. Here are some ideas. Everyone handles difficult emotions differently, so find the ways that feel best for you and practice them!

- Yell or scream into a pillow, or play a musical instrument loudly.
- Listen to music, take 10 deep breaths, leave the situation, or talk it out.
- Walk, run, shoot hoops, hit a pillow, or stomp.
- Draw creatively, squeeze some clay, or journal.

It's never good to destroy property or get physical toward another person. And the sooner you find ways that help you cope with anger and difficult emotions, the better you'll feel. It's never wrong to feel angry. When you can express anger in a way that is healthy and maybe even helpful, other people will respect that and treat you like the mature person you are becoming. Figuring out what works best for you takes time and practice, but it's important and worth it.

Too Difficult? Talk With an Adult

If you find that you are feeling sad, angry, nervous, or frustrated a lot of the time, it is extra important to find someone to talk with. An adult who is a good listener, like a counselor or a family member, is often the most helpful, but sometimes a good friend can help too. If you feel this way most of the time, it's important to tell someone at your doctor's office.

Difficult emotions are a part of life. If you never felt angry or sad, you wouldn't be human. But it's important to realize that these should not be the most common (or only!) emotions you feel.

When You Smile

On the other hand, your "easy" emotions can be fun to express. People love seeing other people happy. Have you ever noticed that when you're happy, smiling, or laughing, your friends want to join you? Sometimes, happiness is *contagious,* meaning your happiness and joy spreads to others.

Or have you ever noticed a time you were in a great mood, but others around you seemed annoyed or frustrated with you? Your happiness might be because you did something awesome and you're feeling proud.

When you feel proud, it's OK to let your happiness shine, but it's also important to let it shine without bragging or rubbing it in. A high five and big smile are great, but acting too proud can be annoying and rude. If you need to brag or celebrate big, save it for when you're in a place where you won't frustrate others who may not be as happy or excited as you are.

Being sensitive to the way other people are feeling is one more part of learning how to deal with your own emotions and express them in healthy and respectful ways around others. That's part of being a good sport and a good friend.

FUN FACT:

Did you know that emotions are contagious? Yep, feelings spread between people, even if we're not paying attention to emotions. So if you're feeling sad and want to feel better, hang out with a group of happy people.

TEASING AND BULLYING

But what happens when kids don't learn how to manage emotions and feelings very well? They may start acting in ways that can be disrespectful or mean to others. This behavior is called *bullying,* and it happens in lots of ways.

Most people think bullying is when someone picks on other people or starts a fight. They might imagine a kid with anger problems and a mean streak. More likely, a kid who bullies can look just like you and even have a lot of friends. Bullying can be physical at times, or it can be emotional by hurting someone's feelings.

Here are some ways that people might bully others.

- Telling a story about someone that isn't true
- Saying mean things about someone to their face or behind their back
- Being in a group that doesn't allow others to join in
- Hurting someone's feelings on purpose
- Whispering or telling secrets in front of others who don't know what you're saying
- Laughing at someone or making a mean comment about someone and claiming it was just a joke or teasing
- Pushing, hitting, slapping, pinching, biting, or hurting someone physically in any way

What does puberty have to do with bullying? The most common reasons kids are bullied or teased is because of body changes or the way they look. Remember that everyone goes through puberty in their own unique way and on their own unique timeline. If you're teasing someone now, you may be the one getting teased later. Has anyone ever told you to treat others the way you want to be treated? That's called the **Golden Rule,** and it's great advice—valuable like pure gold.

Cyberbullies

What about bullies online? You may not have your own computer, tablet, phone, or social media accounts yet, but you probably already know that bullies can sometimes show up online instead of in person. When you begin to use your own devices or social media, it's always a good idea to have a trusted adult help you set up your accounts and check these with you occasionally.

When people write mean or untrue things in social media comments or through texts or direct messages, it's called **cyberbullying.** It can be especially hard to deal with because sometimes their screen name and photo may not be real, so you don't even know who they are or whether they're really who they say they are. Cyberbullying can be written as comments or messages, but it can also be posted as photos of someone without their permission, just to make fun of them or embarrass them. Cyberbullying can be incredibly hurtful.

It's important to understand that cyberbullying is never OK, and if you are being bullied online, it's important to ask a trusted adult for help to make the bullying stop.

But we also know that everyone makes mistakes sometimes, and even the kindest kids can sometimes post a comment that hurts someone's feelings, spreads gossip, or lies. As you're learning how to be a kind person online as well as in real life, it can help to follow these rules when you get your own social media account.

- Don't post a comment that is mean or untrue or that you wouldn't say to someone in person.
- Don't post photos or comments that you wouldn't want your grandparents, parents, or strangers to see.
- Don't trust people online whom you don't know in person.
- Don't text or message things about people that you wouldn't want them to read—your words might be shared.
- Don't take or post photos or videos of anyone without their permission.

Why Bully?

There are a lot of different reasons someone might act mean.

- They may feel jealous.
- They may feel bad about themself and think they will feel better by making you feel bad about yourself.
- They may be copying the way they have been treated by others.
- They may believe that they are powerless and that hurting someone else makes them feel powerful.
- They may think they are being funny.
- They may want attention.

Whatever the reason is for bullying, it's never the funny or right thing to do. Hurting someone's feelings on purpose is just plain wrong. It doesn't feel good for the person being bullied. And the person being mean may even realize that it doesn't make them feel better about themself either.

Nothing feels better than making someone feel great! Want to feel some positive and easy emotions? Make their day! Watch them smile. Laugh with them. Include them in your fun. There's no better way to feel great than to be kind to others. By setting a good example, you will encourage your friends to do the same. It's a win for everyone.

CLIQUES: POSITIVE OR NEGATIVE?

Friends tend to hang out together. Their hanging out is part of friendship. But if you always hang out with the same group of friends, the group may be considered a **clique** (pronounced "click"). Cliques can be positive or negative. Positive groups tend to welcome new friends and work together to do positive things. It's easy to see that a group can do more than one person can when it comes to things like doing projects or helping others.

Then why does the word *clique* seem so negative? When does a group of friends become a problem? The biggest problem with cliques is that the group becomes so tight, it doesn't let others join in its fun. This is called *exclusion,* and it hurts the ones being left out. Remember, exclusion is a type of bullying.

Do you let only certain classmates sit at your lunch table or hang out with you at recess? What if someone outside your group tries to join in? Do you have friends who ignore that person or even leave whenever they come around?

If you have ever been in situations like these, you've seen how exclusion works. There is a kid who is being excluded. There are some people who exclude that kid. And there are **bystanders** who watch this happen but don't really do anything positive OR negative. Even as a bystander, a person can feel bad and not know how to stand up for the one being left out.

BEING IN A CLIQUE IS COMPLICATED

If you have ever stood by and watched another classmate's feelings get hurt by your friends—and wanted to help but didn't—you know that being a bystander is complicated. If you decide to help out the excluded person, your friends may end up excluding you for not sticking by them. If you don't help your classmate, you might feel guilty for not helping. It's normal to have mixed feelings in a situation like this.

How can you keep your friends but still do what feels right? First of all, friends who exclude others are not the best friends to have. One choice is to find another group that isn't so exclusive. Leaving a group that is being mean and finding a better group for you may be really hard, but it may also be really rewarding. What usually happens is that you find the best friends ever in a group that is friendly and kind.

On the other hand, you might be able to help your friends see that it is mean to exclude others. Sometimes people don't even realize that their group is being exclusive or mean. Saying something like "How would you feel by being left out?" can make them more understanding and change the way they act.

What if someone in the group gets mad at you and threatens to never talk with you again or to do something even worse? It's a perfect time to stop being that person's friend. You need to stand up for yourself and speak up for what's right. You need to find your voice, even though it can be scary. If you feel scared or don't know how to stop someone who is bullying you or someone else, talk with a teacher, a parent, or another adult you trust.

FINDING YOUR ANTI–BULLY VOICE

Whether you are being bullied or are just standing by, speaking up takes courage. If you're being bullied, you might just stand there, you might cry, or you may run away. It's hard to speak up for yourself when you're hurt. Having courage can take time and practice. Practice? Yep. It can really help to think about some things you can say if you're bullied or if you're standing by. Following are some suggestions:

What to Say to a Person Who Bullies

- "That's really immature."
- "Stop, think about what you are saying."
- "I'm sorry, you seem to be having a bad day."
- "It's not OK to talk to me like that."
- Say nothing, show no reaction, and just walk away like the bullying had no effect on you.

What to Say if You're a Bystander

- "I can't believe you said that!"
- "How would you feel if someone did that to you?"
- Say the name of the person who bullies in a way that shows you disagree or are surprised at what they are saying, like "Shreya! Why are you doing that?"
- "You need to stop right now. That's not OK here."

BEING A TRUE FRIEND

Being true friends doesn't mean you always have to agree on everything and enjoy the same things. Even the best of friends can have different opinions and different likes and dislikes. What matters in friendship is treating each other well. Remember the Golden Rule? Treat others the way you would like to be treated. It doesn't mean treat others the way they treat you. So you can go first. Think about these true friend practices.

- If you treat others nicely by being helpful and friendly, they will more likely be helpful and friendly to you.
- If you know that you hurt your friend's feelings, be sure to say you are sorry. You would want to be treated the same way if your feelings were hurt.
- If there's a new student in your class, be one of the first to be their friend. You would appreciate someone being your friend if you were new.

Remember, if you treat others in a mean way, you'll get it right back. But if you practice the Golden Rule, you can be a great example for others of how to be a kind and true friend.

FINDING TRUE FRIENDS

Don't expect everyone to be your BFF (best friend forever), and don't feel as if you have to be everyone's best friend. It takes time to grow great friendships. Having even one great friend is better than having a lot of so-so friends. But it's always a great idea to be kind to everyone because you never know who might become your best friend.

Sometimes, best friends are the same gender—for example, girls being friends with girls or boys with boys—and sometimes, they are different genders. Friendships are based on things like being neighbors, having similar interests and hobbies, or playing the same sports. Sometimes kids who have friends of a different gender are teased about having a special someone, like a boyfriend or girlfriend. But this behavior is wrong. Friends are friends. The teasers are wrong and need to stop.

By being a true friend, you will find true friends. True friends bring out the best in you. They are the kids you can talk with and trust. They are honest and stand up for you. They don't talk behind your back. They are happy when things go well for you. They think your weird habits, your goofy laugh, and your crazy hair are just fine. True friends are the ones who know and like the true you.

CRUSHES

As you grow up and get into puberty, you may also notice a special someone who gives you new feelings and whom you like in a different way. You may not even know how to act around them anymore. Most of your friends will stay just that—friends—but sometimes you may start spending more time with someone and get teased about having a special someone, like a girlfriend or boyfriend.

When you get these new feelings of liking someone in a different way, you might have a crush. And it is important to realize, you can't control whom you develop feelings for. They could be another kid in your class, a friend's older sibling, or even your teacher, a coach, or a celebrity. They could be someone whose gender is different from yours or the same.

Do you get sweaty palms around them? Do you do something loud or annoying to get their attention? Or maybe you feel as if you don't know what

to say around your crush anymore. Puberty, brain changes, and hormones may make you act differently around someone you like. If you like someone special, the best way to get noticed is to just be your normal, kind self. Doing goofy and annoying things will get attention, but it's not the kind of attention you want from a crush.

Sometimes your friends or other kids you know may be pressuring you to "like like" a certain person when you really don't have any special feelings for anyone at all. Sometimes those special feelings don't happen until later, when you're a teenager or you're even older. That timeline is normal. There's nothing wrong with you if you don't like someone that way.

Having special feelings for someone and hoping they like you back can be confusing and frustrating, but there's plenty of time to figure it out. Be patient with yourself, be patient with the kids around you, and don't pressure your friends.

GROWING UP

Learning to be a true friend and finding true friends are only a couple of the prizes that come with growing up. Growing up also means managing your emotions, getting really experienced at the things you enjoy doing, being able to do more things by yourself or with your friends, and becoming smarter and smarter. Oh, and of course, growing up also means growing into your new body and feelings with confidence, pride, and a promise to take good care of yourself.

I hope you've learned some things about friendships. I have! In the next chapter, Leshaun is going to help you learn about body parts!

CHAPTER 3

BODY—PART SMARTS

LESHAUN

The boys' locker room at the community center echoes with the sounds of voices and metal locker doors clanging. Antonio, Jack, and I peel off our shirts and shove them into the lockers, ready to head out to the pool in our swim trunks. But just as we're about to leave, Antonio pokes me in the shoulder.

"Isn't that Olivia, from the grade below us?" he asks, not very quietly. I follow Antonio's gaze toward the bathroom stalls. "What is she doing in here? She doesn't have a pee pee."

Jack spits out some of the water he was drinking, dropping the bottle to rest against the arm of his wheelchair. "Did you just say *pee pee*?"

"Well, what do you call it?" I ask, stepping out of Jack's splash zone.

"It's obviously called a *willy*," Jack says, crossing his arms.

"That's my uncle's name," Antonio says, laughing.

"Hey," says a voice behind us, and we all turn to see Olivia's older brother, David. He's wearing his red lifeguard swim trunks, a T-shirt with a whistle around his neck, and a small frown.

I look around quickly, checking that we haven't accidentally broken any of the pool rules. Maybe Jack wasn't supposed to be drinking water in here?

"Oliver was assigned female at birth," David says, and I look back up at him. His expression isn't frowning anymore, just serious.

"That's why you may have known him in the past as Olivia," David continues. "But Oliver is a boy, so that means he's transgender. He belongs in the boys' locker room as much as any of us do."

"Oh," says Antonio, glancing over to where Oliver is stacking his stuff in a locker, "we didn't know."

"It's OK," says David, "now you do. And, in general, not everyone who comes into the boys' locker room will have the same types of body parts. And that's normal."

"I get that," Jack says, patting his legs where they are buckled into his wheelchair.

"So do I," says Antonio, pointing at the giant height difference between him and me.

"Thanks for explaining it to us," I say.

David nods. "No problem. I'm going to tell Oliver I told you, but just make sure you don't tell others—that's his business to tell when he's ready." Then he smiles. "Also, it's called a *penis.*"

"It's a *willy,*" Jack insists, and this time we all laugh.

As we leave the locker room, I notice how everyone we pass is different: shapes, sizes, and colors, dressed in every type of swimsuit imaginable.

"Hey, Oliver," Antonio says when we pass him, "want to play some water basketball with us? Jack and I are so skilled that Leshaun needs a really good teammate, or he won't stand a chance."

Oliver turns, pulling down the edges of his swim shirt, and smiles.

"You're on," he says, and I high-five him.

Because there are a lot of changes going on with your body, you'll want to make sure you know the scoop on all your parts—and all the nicknames you might hear for them, just like Jack has heard "willy"! You already know most of the real names for the parts of your body. You learned most of them when you were a toddler, right? Remember the song "Head, shoulders, knees and toes, knees and toes?" You're singing it now, aren't you? Even babies can point to and name those parts, but what about the parts people don't usually talk about? You know . . . those personal, private, covered-up parts. Yep, *those.*

SILLY NICKNAMES

Can you name all the parts "down there"? Or do you just point to or call the whole area some silly nickname? We've probably heard most of the silly names there are for private parts. People call the **vulva** (VUHL vuh) (Do you know that word yet? If not, you will soon!) things like "pee pee," "hooha," and "pocketbook." And the **penis** has lots of funny names, like "willy," "wiener," "front bump," and "one-eyed snake." What names have you heard?

OK, OK! When you stop laughing, read on.

Besides silly nicknames, there are also some not-so-nice words some people use to describe private parts or things those parts do. You may hear some kids or adults use disrespectful words from time to time. Some kids think they sound cool or older when they use words like those. They don't.

For kids who are in the know, like you, there's no need to use disrespectful or not-so-nice words at all! In fact, using those kinds of words to describe body parts can make those parts seem dirty or wrong. And guess what? There's nothing dirty or wrong about anybody's private parts. Just remember, those parts are there for very important reasons.

Why do people sometimes feel embarrassed or silly when talking about private parts? Maybe they don't know the real names for those parts. Maybe they're just not used to talking about their bodies in a comfortable way. Maybe they've been told *not* to talk about them. Whatever the reason, a lot of people feel awkward when talking about private parts. We want to change that and make sure you feel comfortable with talking about your body.

YOUR PRIVATE PARTS

First, let's talk about why they're referred to as *private parts.*

Basically, everything your swimsuit covers is considered private. And that means nobody should look at or touch those parts except you—and maybe a parent or health care professional if you need help and they have your permission. It also means nobody should ask you to look at or touch *their* private parts or show you any pictures or videos of other people's private parts.

Even though your private parts are private, they're *yours,* and you should know the real names for them, not just nicknames. That way, if you ever have a problem or question about your private parts, you'll know how to talk with a parent, nurse, or doctor. And it will be a lot more comfortable than using silly words!

Ready?

From the Top

Let's start at the top. When we talk about private parts, most people think of the down-there parts. But some people have private parts on top too.

First of all, EVERY body has 2 nipples on their chest.

The **nipple** is the hard little bump inside the circle of darker skin. The circle of darker skin is called the **areola** (a REE oh la or air ee OH la). The areola and the nipple together kind of look like a target, but they can look a bit different on everyone. Some people have nipples that poke out, some lie flat, and some pull inward (that's called **inverted nipples**). Areolae can look different too—dark, light, big, or small, and some have small bumps or hairs around the edges. These are all normal!

FUN FACT:

Some people can have one or more extra nipples on their lower chest. An extra nipple can look a lot like a mole. It's called a **supernumerary nipple,** but it won't grow into an extra breast.

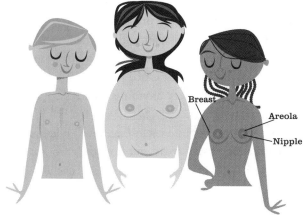

You may already know that during puberty, most girls and kids like Oliver start to develop breasts (we'll get into those details in Chapter 7). Like other ones, these body parts have plenty of nicknames, like "boobs," "bosoms," and "boobies," but the real name is *breasts*. Why do some humans grow

breasts? They're not decorations! Breasts grow to prepare the body for making breast milk, which is the best food there is for a new baby. Whether a person decides to feed their baby breast milk or baby formula depends on a lot of things; sometimes it's just a choice they make. Anyone with ovaries will grow breasts that can make breast milk someday, regardless of whether their breasts are big or small. That's the real reason they are there.

"Down There"

Now let's move to the down-there parts and make sure you know the correct names for EVERY body's parts. You already know some of the names for your own parts, and you might be pretty familiar with them. You also probably have heard the words *penis* and **vagina** (vah JI nuh), but there are a lot more to learn than just those words. All the down-there parts are called **genitals** or **genitalia.**

If you have a penis, you're probably used to seeing it because it dangles right there in front. You can just look down and there it is. You're also probably used to touching and holding your penis because, as a toddler, you learned to aim it into the toilet when you pee.

If you have a vagina, seeing your private parts is a little more challenging. That's because those parts are hidden around a corner and tucked inside some folds between your legs. Also, you've never had to hold your private parts to urinate; you can pee with no hands! Once you learn all the body parts down there, they shouldn't be a mystery anymore, and it's a great idea to take a closer look with a mirror.

As doctors, we know that understanding how bodies work is important. Knowing the names for private parts and how they work can help EVERY body take better care of themselves and understand each other better!

BODY PARTS AND GENDER

Before we dive into everything, though, let's talk about genitals. When you were born, one of the first things the doctor or midwife said was probably "It's a girl!" or "It's a boy!" Why did they say that? They took one look at your genitals and made the announcement. If they said you were a boy, some people probably gave you blue baby clothes. People may have assumed you'd enjoy trucks more than dolls. If they said you were a girl, maybe people around you thought you would enjoy ballet more than baseball or pink more than blue. When people think you automatically like certain colors or things because you've been labeled "boy" or "girl," that's called a **gender stereotype.**

It's a baby!

Of course, stereotypes are not always true because every person is unique.

So here's the thing: your private parts don't decide what you like to do, what you like to wear, or who you are on the inside. They have nothing to do with what sports you get to play, what friends you choose, or what color shoes you wear. YOU get to determine all those for yourself!

FUN FACT:

Until the early 1900s, parents dressed all children in white until they were about 6 years old. Then parents started dressing boys in pink because it was considered a stronger, more masculine color. They dressed girls in blue because it was considered a more delicate and feminine color. Around 1940, the color choices for girls and boys flipped, making blue popular for boys and pink for girls. Today, we know colors don't have a gender!

So here's the deal: when someone looks at a baby's genitals and says, "It's a girl," or "It's a boy," that's called their **sex assigned at birth** because, well, it *is* assigned at birth. Make sense? If a baby is born with a penis, their sex assigned at birth is male. If a baby is born with a vulva, their sex assigned at birth is female. And some babies are born with genitals that aren't clearly either a penis and scrotum or a vulva. These babies are assigned a different sex at birth, called **intersex.** The reasons for intersex are very complicated and are related to hormones or genes or to differences that happen during development before birth.

Most babies who are born with a penis grow up feeling like a boy on the inside too. That's called being **cisgender** (*cis-* means "same"). But there are some babies born with a penis who grow up feeling like a girl on the inside. That's called being **transgender** (*trans-* means "cross" or "opposite"). Similarly, if a baby born with a vulva grows up feeling like a girl, she is a cisgender girl. If that baby grows up knowing he is a boy, then he is a transgender boy. Did you notice here that we said *he* instead of *she*? This is a baby who was born with a vulva but feels like a boy on the inside. So instead of saying *she,* as we often do for kids born with a vulva, we say *he,* because that's who this person truly is, on the inside. The most important thing is to respect the way a person feels on the inside by using the pronouns they ask you to use.

And for some kids, they aren't sure whether they feel more like a girl, a boy, a bit of both, or neither; they just feel different. Sometimes it just takes time to figure out how you feel, and that's normal too. Knowing and feeling that you're a boy, a girl, a little bit of both, or not really either (no matter what genitals you have) is called your **gender identity.**

FUN FACT:

A pronoun is a word we use to describe someone in a way that's shorter than their name. The most common pronouns are *she/her/hers, he/him/his,* and *they/them/theirs.* Pronouns match someone's gender identity.

GENDER DIVERSITY

It's OK if figuring out how you feel seems a little confusing. If you've never thought about this, you're probably cisgender and your genitals likely match how you feel on the inside. But some kids have confusing, frustrating, or sad thoughts about how their body doesn't feel quite right for them.

Remember how we said there are no wrong feelings and you can't help the way you feel about things? Your gender identity is also like that: you can't help the way you feel, and there's no wrong or right way to be when it comes to gender identity. You are who you are, and that's what makes the world full of so many unique and interesting people. If you're not feeling OK about who you are, it's important to tell a doctor, a therapist, or another trusted adult who can help you. When people understand that nobody can change the way they feel inside, and every single person is important and valuable, then the world is easier and better for EVERY body.

More Than Two

Many people think there are only 2 genders—boy and girl. That way of thinking is called the **gender binary.** The word **binary** means having only 2 parts, so *gender binary* means there are only boys and girls. But guess what? There are actually more than 2 gender identities. Transgender is one we've already mentioned, but there are lots of ways people describe their gender. The term **gender diverse** covers all the gender identities that are not cisgender. The following box lists words people may use to describe gender identity:

cisgender—This word describes people whose sex assigned at birth is the same as the gender they feel on the inside. Most people are cisgender.

gender diverse—This word describes all the gender identities that are not cisgender.

transgender—This word describes people whose sex assigned at birth is different from the gender they feel on the inside.

nonbinary—This word describes people who don't feel like either a girl or a boy on the inside, or they may feel like some of both. Because people who are nonbinary don't feel like a girl or a boy, they may not be comfortable with being called *he* or *she*. Instead, they may prefer to be called *they* (even though they are one person). Or they may use a special pronoun, like *xe* or *ze* (both pronounced "zee").

bigender—This word describes people who feel like they are both a boy and a girl on the inside.

gender fluid—This word describes people who feel like a girl sometimes and a boy sometimes or who may at times feel like neither.

There are lots of words to describe how diverse gender can be! A lot of people think this is a new idea, but there have been gender-diverse people noted throughout history. There are also cultures all over the world that have gender identities other than just boys and girls. The world is full of so many interesting people!

So, can you look at someone and know whether they are gender diverse? Nope. The way someone looks on the outside, like their hairstyle and clothes, is called their **gender expression.** If someone has long hair or wears makeup and dresses, those would be considered a **feminine** gender expression in most cultures. Lots of people think that if someone has a feminine gender expression, they must be a girl. But that's another stereotype. Similarly, when someone expresses themself by wearing jerseys, baseball caps, or short hair, it's called a **masculine** gender expression. Someone's gender expression might give us a clue to their gender identity, but you can't know for sure someone's gender identity by how they look on the outside.

Now that you know what sex assigned at birth, gender identity, and gender expression are, you can see where the characters in the stories feel like they belong on the chart on page 32. You can also think about where you would put yourself!

If You Have a Vagina

So let's get back to body parts and start with outside private parts that most girls, some nonbinary kids, and kids like Oliver have. If you have these parts, you know some of the names for them. If you don't have these parts, it's a great time to learn more about them!

The first thing to learn is that there is one name for the group of parts down there. The whole area between the legs is called the **vulva** (VUHL vuh). Just like a face has other, smaller parts, like eyes, a nose, and cheeks, the vulva includes a lot of different parts too. And now that you know the name, you can stop calling those outside parts a vagina!

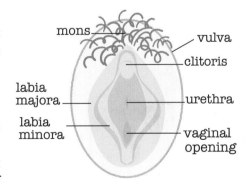

You·ology

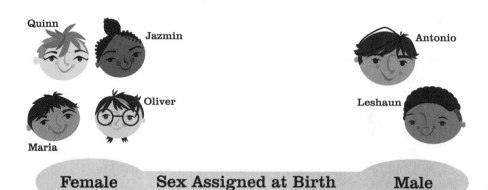

If you have a vulva, and you look down to try to see what's there, the main thing you can see is a fatty bump called the **mons** (pronounced "monz"). It's fatty and soft to protect the bone that is underneath. It's also the place where pubic hair will grow.

Below the mons and between the legs, there are 2 flaps or folds that meet in the middle. They are mostly closed but can be spread open, kind of like lips. And guess what they are called? Large lips. Well, sort of! In Latin, the word for "lips" is *labia,* and the word for "big" is *majora.* The real name for those flaps or folds is **labia majora** (LAY be uh ma JOR uh). They are the larger lips that cover some other sensitive parts between them.

Now, if the labia majora are spread apart, there are other folds of skin in there. They are called the **labia minora** (LAY be uh mi NOR ah). I bet you can figure out what that means. *Labia* means "lips." *Minora* means "minor" or "smaller." You got it! They're the smaller, or inner, lips that also help protect other sensitive parts.

At the top of the labia minora is a bump called the **clitoris** (CLIT or us). The bump is just the tip of the clitoris. The rest of the clitoris is larger, but it is inside the body, under the skin of the labia and vagina. The clitoris holds tons of nerves that make it feel tingly or tickly when it's touched. If you have a clitoris, you may have already discovered that touching it can feel good. The clitoris is the part of the vulva that is most sensitive to touch. The tip of a penis is sensitive in a similar way.

FUN FACT:

Even though *labia minora* means "smaller lips," they grow a lot during puberty and can become longer than the labia majora. Labia minora look different from person to person, just like our faces! Some are long and poking out; some are short and tucked in. One may be longer than the other. They can also be wrinkly, smooth, pinkish, or brownish. There is no right or wrong way for them to look!

Between the labia minora are 2 holes or openings. The hole closest to the clitoris is the opening where urine (pee) comes out. It's called the **urethra** (your REE thra), and it can also be pretty sensitive to touch or chemicals.

The hole below or behind the urethra is the opening to the **vagina** (vah JI nuh). It's not only the opening where most babies come out (surprise!) but also the part that connects the outside parts to the inside parts.

When it comes to the vaginal opening, we know you're probably wondering, "How can a whole baby fit through there?" We know that doesn't seem possible, but when someone is pregnant and starts to have a baby (that's called being in **labor**), the vagina can stretch and stretch to be big enough to let a baby out. Its ability to stretch is one more cool thing about our bodies!

If a baby can't be delivered through the vagina, there is one other way they can come out: through a type of surgery called a **cesarean delivery** (also called a **C-section**). During a C-section, a doctor cuts an opening through the lower part of the belly into the **uterus** (YOU ter us) (more on that later on in this chapter) to take the baby out. There are different reasons why someone might need a C-section, but most babies are born through the vagina. Whichever way babies get here, it's always amazing!

Last, there is one more opening down there, but it's not considered part of the vulva because EVERY body has one. It's the hole you have a bowel movement (poop) through, and it's called the **anus.** You may notice that some kids giggle when the science teacher talks about the planets and mentions "Uranus." Uranus is a gassy planet (Get it?). Your science teacher may even giggle. Something about that word just makes us laugh sometimes. It's OK! Bodies can be funny sometimes. We just want to make sure you know the correct words for all your parts.

So finally, if you have a vulva, now that you know all about your genitals, we think it's a great idea to grab a mirror and take a look! No need to be shy, they are *your* parts. Find a private place with good lighting, or you may want to use a flashlight. It's definitely something to do alone because your genitals are private. You need to know what your genitals look like, and you'll feel better knowing you have all the parts you are learning about.

It's normal and healthy to be curious about your own body, and understanding your body is important as you learn to take care of yourself. If you have any questions or worries, you might want to ask a parent or your doctor. Being able to go to an adult you trust with your questions and worries is important.

If You Have a Penis

Let's shift to talking about the genitals that most boys and some nonbinary or transgender kids, like Kimi, have.

If you were born with a penis, you've been looking at and touching it since you were a baby, right? And at some point (hopefully a long time ago!), you learned to hold your penis to aim it into the toilet when you pee. So if you're like most kids with a penis, you have been pretty familiar with your genitals for a long time, and you know the names too, but let's go through them just to be sure. If you don't have a penis, it's still important to learn about these parts to understand how EVERY body works!

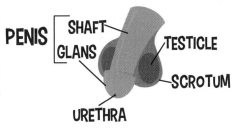

The penis is the body part where pee (urine) comes out. It hangs down in front of the body. It has 2 parts: the **glans** (also called the *head*), which is the tip of the penis, and the **shaft,** which is the longer part that attaches to the body. At the tip of the penis is an opening where urine comes out, and it's called the *urethra.* EVERY body has a urethra because EVERY body pees.

Behind and hanging below the penis are 2 testes that some kids call "balls" or "nuts."

If you're talking about two, they are called *testes* or *testicles.* But one is just called a *testicle* (not a test!). In humans, both testes are about the same size. During puberty, they will grow and one will hang lower than the other. After puberty, the average testicle is about 2 inches long and 1 inch wide.

Testosterone is made in the testes and sent out to the body from there. Testes are also the place where a special type of cell, called **sperm,** is made. We talk more about sperm later in this chapter.

The testes hang in a pouch of thin skin called the **scrotum.** As puberty progresses, the scrotum will stretch and hang a little lower as the testes grow, and it will also get darker in color. This little sack may seem simple, but it has some pretty special powers as a thermostat (that means it helps control the temperature of your testes). Why would it need to do that? Don't worry, we answer that question in Chapter 9.

Finally, like we said before, because EVERY body poops, there's also an anus down there. Some people call it a *butthole,* but now you know the correct word for it.

CIRCUMCISION

Have you ever heard the word **circumcision** (sir come SIH shun)? Everyone born with a penis has a piece of skin, called the **foreskin,** that covers the glans of the penis. Some parents choose to have their child's foreskin removed, and that is called *circumcision.*

When someone is circumcised, their foreskin is removed by a doctor (or mohel in the Jewish faith). It's most common to have this done soon after birth. Some parents choose to leave the foreskin as is. Occasionally, there may be a medical reason why a baby can't be circumcised, but a person can be circumcised at any age. There are a lot of different reasons why parents may or may not choose circumcision for their child. So it's normal if a penis is circumcised, and it's normal if it's not. Even though a circumcised penis looks a bit different from an uncircumcised one, it works just the same.

If you have an uncircumcised penis, you'll need to pay a little more attention to cleaning it. When you take a bath or shower, you should gently pull back your foreskin to clean under it. If soap stings, just use water. If you can't pull your foreskin back very far, that's OK. Over time, it will loosen up, and you will be able to pull it all the way back when you get older. Don't ever force your foreskin back if it hurts. If it ever feels tight or if it becomes red or swollen, tell your parent or trusted adult, and see your doctor.

Circumcised　　　　　　　　**Uncircumcised**

So for kids with a penis, the outside private parts are simple. But as puberty begins, things will start to change on the outside and on the inside.

WHAT'S GOING ON IN THERE?

Inside parts? Yep! You know how we named all the outside parts of the genitals? There are also inside parts that work with those outside parts. Like other inside parts (like your brain, heart, and lungs), even though you can't see them, they're in there to do important jobs. As you go through puberty, you'll start to know they're working by the new things going on with your body. Are you ready to learn the names of those parts too? We share more about what they do in chapters 8 and 9.

Remember that one reason EVERY body goes through puberty is so they can help make baby humans in the future. The genitals, and the inside parts connected to them, usually do 1 of 2 things. If you have a penis, your body can provide the **sperm** cell that is needed to make a baby. If you have a vulva, your body provides a different cell, called an **egg** (human eggs are not like chicken eggs!) that is needed to make a baby. Your body also has a safe place to grow a baby until it is ready to be born! Let's learn all the names for those cool inside parts.

more inside parts

A Baby-Growing Body

Most girls and kids like Oliver have some pretty cool inside parts that work together. First, remember how we talked about the opening to the vagina? The vagina is actually a soft tunnel that starts at the vulva and goes inside the body to connect the inside parts to the outside world (That's how a baby is born!).

On the inside, the vagina ends at something called the **cervix** (SIR vix), which is like a dead end but has a teeny-tiny tunnel that leads into the next part, called the *uterus*. The uterus is like a ball of muscle with a thick shell but a soft, hollow space in the middle. The inside layer of the uterus is called the **endometrium** (en do ME tree um). Then, there are 2 things that look like long arms that come off the top of the uterus. They are called **fallopian** (fa LOW pee an) **tubes.** Finally, near the end of each fallopian tube is an oval-shaped **ovary** (OH ver ee).

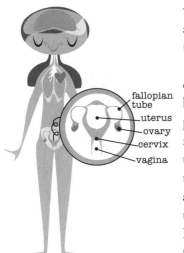

fallopian tube
uterus
ovary
cervix
vagina

There's one on each side, and they're each about the size of a walnut. The ovaries hold the eggs that are needed to help make a baby.

The uterus deserves a little more attention because it has some special powers. Think about its important jobs.

The uterus can grow a baby, stretch as the baby grows bigger, and then push a big baby out of that small vaginal opening. Those obviously take great muscle strength, and guess what? The uterus is made of amazingly strong and coordinated muscles!

strong!   strong!

really,
really
strong!

> **FUN FACT:**
> Females are born with about 1 million eggs in each ovary.

When it comes time for a baby to be born, the uterus squeezes and relaxes and then squeezes and relaxes. When it does so over and over again, it begins to push the baby out. The squeezes are called **contractions,** and when the uterus works super hard to push that big baby out of that little opening, it's called labor. There's nothing stronger than a uterus!

A Sperm-Making Body

Most boys and kids like Kimi have bodies that can make sperm, and the penis is involved. Do you wonder how? We already mentioned that urine travels in the urethra as it passes through the penis and out of the body. But guess what *also* comes out through the urethra? Sperm.

The cool thing is that urine and sperm come from very different places inside the body. Urine is made by the kidneys and then sent into the bladder to be stored. When the bladder is full, it can squeeze to send the urine out of the urethra. Even though sperm also leave the body through the urethra, sperm have their own place where they're made and stored. Sperm also have their own pathway to get into the urethra and out of the body so they don't pass through the bladder. That means nobody can pee and have sperm come out at the same time. The inside parts make sure the urethra is doing only one job at a time. We explain that more in Chapter 9.

> **FUN FACT:**
> One sperm is a sperm. Two sperm cells are not called *sperms;* they're sperm too. *Sperm* is the plural word for sperm.

Let's talk about the parts that make the sperm and how sperm leaves the body. You already know sperm are made in the testes, but did you know that a couple of years into puberty, each testicle starts making sperm—actually, millions of sperm—every single day? Sperm are obviously extremely tiny.

After sperm are made, they move to a storage area above each testicle called the **epididymis** (epi DID uh mus). Each epididymis is a small and tightly coiled tube where sperm finish growing and learn to swim.

To get out of the body, the sperm leave the epididymis and travel through a long tube called the **vas deferens** (vas DEF er ehns). There's one coming from each testicle. Each vas deferens travels around the bladder and connects with the urethra on the inside of the body.

Along the way, the vas deferens also passes a couple of small glands, including the **prostate gland.** These glands add fluids to the sperm, and when the sperm mix with these fluids, the new mixture is called **semen** (SEA men). The added fluids help the sperm swim easier and provide nutrients for energy. They're kind of like the drinks and snacks you might want on a long hike. It's a loooooong trip for those tiny sperm, so they have to work hard to travel all the way to the end!

Bladder

Vas Deferens

Prostate Gland

Testicle

FUN FACT:
Starting in puberty, the male body makes several million sperm every day—about 1,500 per second.

INSIDE OUT AND OUTSIDE IN

Now that you know all about your outside parts and your inside parts, you know that your private parts are a lot more than just a vulva or a penis! There are so many other parts that work with your private parts. Although your body may seem a bit complicated, what a miraculous thing it is! You are made incredibly well, and your body can do special and amazing things. You may not always feel so great about your body parts, especially as they change. But when you look at all your parts and how they work together to do such cool and extraordinary things, you'll just have to smile from your head, to your shoulders, to your knees and toes!

Whew! That's a lot of body parts! Now let's talk about other stuff that happens in puberty...like hair! Take it away, Stephanie!

CHAPTER 4

HELLO, HAIRY

STEPHANIE

When I open the front door, I'm immediately greeted by a tiny ball of fur wagging and happily barking.

"Good boy, Champ!" I lean down to pet his soft puppy fur and scoop him up into my arms. "I told you I'd be back." Champ licks me all over my face like he hasn't seen me in thousands of years.

"How was the pool?" Mom asks, planting a kiss of her own on my head. She's still wearing her suit from work, but I see the flurry of dog hair on the black fabric, evidence of cuddles with Champ.

"It was good," I say. "Shreya and Maria taught me how to swim backstroke. And then we ran into some of the boys from school—Antonio, Leshaun, Oliver, and Jack. They invited us to play water basketball with them, but I was too embarrassed."

"About what?" Mom says. Champ squirms in my arms, and I set him on the ground to run off again.

I sigh. "When I was swimming backstroke with Shreya and Maria, I guess they saw the hair under my arms. We started talking about it, since Maria doesn't really have hair there yet, and Shreya says she shaves hers. She offered to teach me how, but I was kind of embarrassed. And I didn't want anyone else to see it while we played water basketball."

Mom reaches out to touch my red curls, tucking a strand behind my ear. "I'm sorry, honey. Your hair is so beautiful! You should never be embarrassed by it."

"I guess the hair under my arms feels a little less beautiful," I shrug. "And Shreya shaves her legs too. Should I be doing that?"

"You should be shaving whatever makes you feel the most comfortable," Mom says. She points to her dark, bushy eyebrows. "Some people like to get their eyebrows waxed or plucked, but I never have! It's all about personal choice. And hair grows back, so you can always change your mind. Your dad had a beard for our first few years of dating, and now he shaves it. But he could always grow it back if he wanted to."

I try to imagine Dad with a beard and then shake my head vigorously. "No, thanks. I like him without a beard."

Mom laughs. "Me too. But he gets to decide. That's part of what's fun about growing up—you get to make these choices for yourself, based on what makes you feel best."

"I think shaving my armpits might make me feel best," I say. "But I don't think I'm ready to do anything else yet."

Mom nods. "I'll show you tonight, if you want. I have a new razor and some shaving cream you can use. I think you'll be amazed at how quickly you get the hang—"

Champ interrupts her by barking and zooming into the room, showing me his new, colorful rope toy and pushing it against my ankles. I laugh.

"And look how cute Champ is, covered in fur!" Mom says. "There's nothing wrong with being hairy and happy."

"He *is* hairy and happy," I agree. "And cute!" Champ barks in agreement, and when I reach down to grab his toy to play, I let my underarm hair show, and I don't care at all.

Remember the definition of *puberty*, "to grow hairy or mossy"? Once you hit puberty, that hair growth starts in some new places on your body. How much hair you grow depends a lot on your **biological parents** (the 2 people who provided the egg and sperm to make you) and the genes you inherit from them and their ancestors. Where you sprout hair depends on—you guessed it—hormones.

We mentioned in Chapter 1 that EVERY body begins to make the hormone testosterone early in puberty. Testicles make a lot. Ovaries make a little. Even a little testosterone will cause EVERY body to grow darker, thicker hair on their legs; in their armpits; around their private parts; around their nipples; or on their face. Testosterone is the hormone that makes you grow new hairs and makes them darker, thicker, and sometimes curly. The amount of testosterone you have determines how much and where the hair shows up.

If you have a lot of testosterone, you will grow more hair on your face—maybe a mustache-, beard-, or sideburn-type of hair. You might also (later in puberty) grow hair on your chest, abdomen (belly), and back.

Everyone grows body hair in new places, and everyone can decide for themself if they like it or if they don't. The cool thing about hair is that the way it looks is easy to change. You can let it grow, change the color or length, or remove it completely. And if you change your mind, you can change your hair again because it keeps growing back.

HOW THE "PUBES" PROGRESS

The good news is that all that new hair won't sprout overnight. Phew! The hair that grows around your genitals is called **pubic hair** (some kids may call it "pubes"). It shows up slowly and spreads in a pattern that's pretty similar for everyone. Doctors describe how much pubic hair you have from stages 1 to 5. These stages help them know where you are in the puberty process, and that helps them tell you what to expect next. Here's how the stages flow.

Stage 1: Nothing really, just some peach fuzz at the base of the penis or on the labia and mons (Not sure what those are? Head back to Chapter 3).

Stage 2: Darker, longer hairs begin to grow at the base of the penis or on the labia or mons. There are only a few at first, and you can count them (if you want). That means if you can say "Hey! I have 4 pubic hairs!" you are in stage 2. Congratulations!

Stage 3: At this stage, there is more hair. The hair becomes curlier, and it is spreading around the base of the penis or across the labia and mons. Here's how you know you've progressed to stage 3: you could probably count each hair if you really wanted to, but the counting would take a long time!

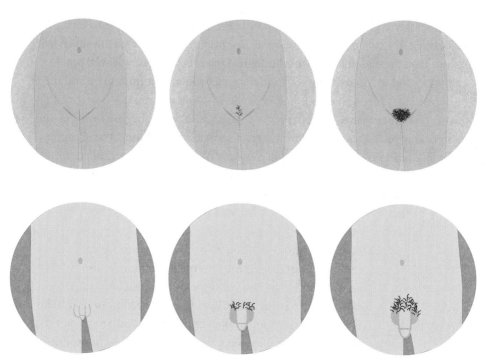

Stage 4: Once you arrive at stage 4, the pubic hair has filled in a lot and there's no way you would want to count the hairs! The hair fills in around the base of the penis or in the shape of a triangle on the mons.

Stage 5: The last stage of pubic hair growth is called an *adult pattern* (even though you're not an adult yet!), which means the hair can spread up toward your belly button, down onto your thighs, and between your legs toward your anus.

So there you have it: the facts on pubic hair. Everyone has it, but some people have more or less than others. The color of your pubic hair is usually a little darker than your head hair. If you have red hair, yours will be reddish. If you have blonde or brown hair, yours will likely be light or dark brown. And if you have black hair, it will be black.

THERE'S A PURPOSE FOR PUBES

As weird as it may seem to grow hair in private places, pubic hair is there for a reason. The skin on your genitals is delicate and sensitive to things like detergents, scents, and even rubbing from underwear and clothing. The pubic hair is like padding and protection for that sensitive skin. And for kids with a vulva, it does one other important thing. Keep reading to find out!

NEW STUFF "DOWN THERE"

Just like the estrogen released from ovaries signals the body to start growing breasts (see Chapter 1), it also causes some changes "down there" on the vulva and in the vagina. Around the same time that breasts start budding, estrogen also signals the vagina to start making more fluids that look like creamy white or yellowish stuff, which is called **vaginal discharge.** Vaginal discharge is very normal, and it's supposed to be there! At first, though, it may be a little uncomfortable or embarrassing because it can feel wet, and sometimes a little sticky, in your underwear.

You may be wondering why the vagina even makes discharge. Believe it or not, it's the way the vagina cleans itself. That's why there's never any need to clean inside the vagina (but remember, the vulva is different; it's an outside part that should be cleaned). The discharge can change sometimes too. It can be thin and watery; clear, slimy, and mucousy (like snot from your nose); or thick and creamy. Once it oozes out of the vagina (it's only a very little at a time), it can make underwear a little bit wet, or it can dry up and be kind of crusty and yellowish. It has a smell but isn't stinky. It can also stain your underwear yellowish or remove some of the dye from darker underwear. That's something that happens to anyone with vaginal discharge, but it's not something people usually talk about. Now you know it's normal!

FUN FACT: Vaginal discharge is made of water, fluids from the cervix, cells, and healthy bacteria. Just like your mouth has saliva, and your eyes have tears, your vagina has discharge.

TAKE CARE DOWN THERE

When vaginal discharge first starts, it can sometimes irritate the sensitive skin on the vulva, making it red and itchy. You or your parent may worry you have an infection, but the redness and itchiness are almost always skin irritation. Once the pubic hair fills in on the mons and vulva, the hair helps pull the discharge away from the skin and makes it less irritating. See? There's a purpose for the pubes!

If you have vaginal discharge but not much hair, you may want to use a small pad, called a **panty liner** (see Chapter 8), to absorb the discharge. You can also put some diaper rash cream (or an over-the-counter ointment with zinc oxide) on your vulva to protect the skin from being bothered by the discharge. Your vulva will feel better once the skin has hair or you keep the discharge off with a cream or pad.

MORE HAIR HERE AND THERE

Pubic hair usually grows before you may notice more hair in other places, like your legs, armpits, and face. If you have dark hair and light skin, your new hair may be more obvious. If your hair color and skin color are similar, you may not even notice the new hair until there's a lot. Every single hair that you grow in puberty is absolutely normal, no matter what it looks like, but what you decide to do with it is absolutely your choice.

Maybe you can't wait to have hairy legs and grow a mustache! Maybe you want silky smooth legs. Sometimes there's pressure from others to get rid of hair, especially if you're a girl, but it's more important that you do what feels most comfortable for you. Doing nothing is perfectly fine and super easy! If you are bothered by the hair, you might feel better if you remove it.

HAIR BE GONE!

There are several ways to remove unwanted hair, but there isn't one way that works best for everyone. That means you may have to try a couple of different methods to see what works best for you and your hair. Sometimes the easiest or safest way to remove the unwanted hair depends on where it's growing.

Body Hair Removal

Shaving

The most common way people handle the hair on body parts like their legs and armpits is to shave it off. So do you just grab someone's razor and get to work? No way! It's very important to use your very own razor. Sharing a razor with someone else can spread bacteria and cause skin infections.

FUN FACT:

Your entire body (except for the palms of your hands and the soles of your feet) is covered in hair. You have about 5 million follicles, about the same as the monkey species. That number never changes, but hairs may fall out of follicles and never grow back.

But, before you grab your razor, there's something else you need: clean skin!

When you wash your skin with soap and water, you remove bacteria that can cause skin irritation or infections. Next, it's helpful to apply shaving cream or more soap to create a good frothy lather. That helps lift the hairs off the skin so they are easier to shave off.

If you press down too hard with the razor, or try to shave dry or dirty skin, you can end up with itchy red bumps on the area called *razor rash*. That's no fun! You can prevent this rash by using a fresh, clean razor; making sure the skin is slick with soapy water or shaving cream; and learning how to hold and use the razor gently. The first time you shave, it's great to have some help from a trusted adult or older sibling who can show you how to avoid cuts.

Once you start shaving, the hair usually starts growing back in a few days. As it grows back, it will feel stiffer and a little prickly. Some people shave about once a week, but others shave more often. Other people shave only during the summer when they wear shorts or swimsuits. If you decide to stop shaving, the hair will eventually become soft again, but this change may take a few weeks, maybe longer. That's why some grown-ups recommend that you wait, because once you start shaving, if you want to stay smooth and hair-free, you'll need to keep shaving pretty regularly.

Waxing or Creams

There are other ways to get rid of unwanted hair on your legs and armpits—and even on your arms, belly, back and chest—but most of those are best for when you're older. Waxing and depilatory (hair removal) creams work for some people. *Waxing* means hot wax is put on your skin where the unwanted hair is, then fabric goes on top of the wax. Once the wax cools a little, the fabric is ripped off quickly and it pulls all the hair out by the roots. Owie! The depilatory creams have strong chemicals that can dissolve hair. Neither of these methods are great for young, sensitive skin because the hot wax can burn the skin, or the chemicals can cause blisters or skin rashes.

FUN FACT:

Hair can grow 0.4 millimeters per day in its growing phase. Hormones control how long the growing phase lasts. Leg hairs grow for about 2 months, which is why they are short. Armpit hairs make it to 6 months, but head hairs grow nonstop for 6 years or more.

    If you want to try something other than shaving, check with a parent or trusted grown-up.

Facial Hair Removal

Did you know that all kids grow new hair on their face at puberty, especially on the upper lip in the mustache area? Yep. Many girls do too. That's because EVERY body makes testosterone during puberty—some bodies more than others. And once again, how you handle that hair is totally up to you.

For Most Boys

Facial hair usually shows up first on your upper lip as a soft, wispy mustache. It will probably start to sprout on your chin and near your ears as sideburns. The hairless spots will eventually fill in as you move through puberty. If you decide you want to shave your facial hair (most kids don't have enough facial hair to shave until middle school or high school), and you're going to use a razor, there are definitely some things to know before you start.

1. **Ask for help.** You'll probably do best if you can ask a parent, an older sibling, or another trusted and experienced shaver to help you learn how to shave carefully and correctly.

2. **Use your own razor.** We gave this advice once already, but it's important: never ever ever ever ever ever use anyone else's razor. Razors can make tiny cuts and pick up blood and skin bacteria that can be passed from one person to another. That bacteria can cause skin infections and even pass along dangerous viruses you don't want.

3. **Clean your skin and lather up.** Wash your face before you shave, and use shaving cream. These 2 things will help prevent small cuts or red bumps and irritated skin.

If a normal razor seems a little complicated or scary, some people prefer to start with an electric razor, which can be a lot easier, as well as less risky for cuts, and there's no need for shaving cream!

Finally, some grown-ups use aftershave or cologne after shaving. Sometimes, these can be harsh on young skin and cause burning or pimples. They can also have a really strong smell! If you want to try someone else's aftershave or cologne, be sure to ask them first.

For Most Girls

There are some girls, especially those with dark hair, who will grow facial hair during puberty. It is very common above the upper lip in the mustache area but can also show up in the sideburn area or on the bottom of the chin. In some cultures, people don't make a big deal about this type of facial hair. In other situations, sadly, it can be a reason for teasing or bullying.

Facial hair is a normal part of puberty, and teasing someone about it is never OK. Their hair is their business. But if *your* hair bothers *you,* there are different ways to manage it. It's always good to ask a parent or trusted adult for help.

Anyone can shave their facial hair if they want to, whether they have a lot or a little. But we *don't* recommend using the same type of razor you

use on your legs or armpits. When you don't expect a lot of facial hair, the easiest and safest way to remove facial hair is with a mini electric razor that has a small tip, or "head," made for small areas like those above your lip.

A lot of people worry that shaving facial hair will make it grow back thicker, stubbly, and darker. It won't! Once you shave, the hair that grows back might feel stiffer, but if you don't have testes producing a lot of testosterone, the hair won't grow in thick. Usually, you have to remove facial hair only once every couple of weeks. If you want to try a mini electric razor, just make sure you ask an adult for help the first time.

Plucking, Waxing, or Creams

Just like with body hair, there are many other ways to handle facial hair. The list is long: plucking, waxing, depilatory creams, bleaching, laser treatments, threading, and even prescription creams that stop hair from growing. Because faces are even more sensitive than skin in other places, and younger skin can become irritated or burned a lot easier than adult skin, it's always important to seek help from a parent, a trusted adult, or even your doctor if you are interested in some of these other methods. Many of them are safer for adults than for young people.

FUN FACT:
It's normal to lose about 70 to 100 hairs from your head every day.

Pubic Hair Removal

A lot of kids ask about removing pubic hair because maybe they've noticed a parent or an older sibling who does that. Why? It's totally a personal choice, but as doctors, we want you to know, there's no need to shave the hair, wax it, or remove it. But some people are bothered by it or want to adjust it just a little. If it pokes out of your swimsuit and bothers you, there are several ways to remove it, but removal can be tricky. We recommend removing or trimming only the hairs that are out of bounds (not all the hairs) and asking your parent or trusted adult to give you some tips on how to do it safely. If they're not sure, talk with your doctor about the best way for you.

And if your pubic hair just seems too long, you can trim it with some scissors. But be very careful: seeing everything down there can be hard. Don't trim the hair too close, or you might unintentionally cut your skin. Ouch! There's no reason to ever remove all of it because it has a purpose, right?

This may seem like one of the craziest parts of puberty. Pubic hair is not something we chat about a lot, partly because what you do with it is totally up to you, not anyone else. Sometimes, though, you just need to know that all these changes are normal. Welcome to this stage of puberty!

Now that we know it's normal to grow new hair, Jack is ready to tell you about another new puberty thing—odors!

CHAPTER 5

BEATING BODY ODORS

JACK

I s it just me," I ask as Antonio joins me in the back of the bus, "or does this bus smell terrible?"

Antonio slides into the seat across the aisle, wrinkling his nose. "It's not just you."

I look toward the front, where I see kids making similar faces and even coughing as they settle into their seats with their instrument cases. It's only supposed to be a 10-minute drive to our band performance at the downtown theater. But this smell is making 10 minutes feel like a very long time.

"OK, everyone!" calls Mr Bellows, our after-school band director, as he steps onto the bus with his clipboard. His dark mustache curves upward with his usual enthusiastic smile. "I hope you're all ready to have a great show today! Together, we will show your friends and family the beauty of the music we have learned together. We will show them how many different instruments can come together to form one beautiful creation! A rainbow of sound, a chorus of emotion, a symbol of the beauty of working in harmony with one another, thousands of individual notes become one magnificent—"

"Uh, Mr Bellows?" Kimi pipes up from the row in front of us. Her fingers are pinching her nose shut, making her voice sound funny. "It really stinks in here."

The bus echoes with laughter, with a few coughs to add to her point.

"Ah!" says Mr Bellows, somehow excited by this fact. "Music is a labor of love! You will work hard! You may sweat! You may even cry with joy!"

"I don't think joy is what's making my eyes water right now," Kimi whispers to me, still plugging her nose.

"Therefore," Mr Bellows continues, "it is important, as musicians and as citizens of the world, to wash yourselves regularly. To use soap. To use deodorant. Just as we polish our instruments, we must also take care of the beautiful instruments of life that are our bodies!"

On top of the stink, the bus is now filled with eye rolls.

"Are we there yet?" someone asks.

"I wish!" Kimi replies.

One of the big responsibilities of puberty is learning to take care of your changing body. You definitely don't need anyone to bathe you or dress you anymore, but with all these new changes, you could probably use some tips for keeping your body fresh and feeling good! Think about all the changes of puberty: new hair, more sweat and oil, morphing private parts, and even new smells. These changes may sound like a lot to handle, or maybe they sound exciting. Either way, with a little daily attention, you'll be a pro at taking care of you!

READY, SET—TY, SWEATY!

What's the big deal about sweat? All your life, you've been sweating. But here's the deal: in puberty, you'll sweat more than ever. Sometimes you'll sweat because you are hot or exercising, but in puberty, you may also sweat because you are feeling nervous, because you are feeling emotional, or sometimes just because.

Sweating is an important way your body stays cool. Your body works best at a temperature of 98.6 °F. To make sure you stay close to that temperature, your body has special ways to keep itself there.

Here's how it works: when you get hot, your brain sends signals to your body to start sweating. Sweat is mostly water, and that is why it makes your skin feel wet. As the water leaves your skin through evaporation, it takes the extra heat away, and you feel cooler. Sweat by itself doesn't really have an odor, but keep reading to see what happens with your sweat during puberty.

FUN FACT:
If you could collect all the sweat you make in 1 day, you would be amazed! During puberty, if you're well hydrated and exercising really hard, you can sweat enough in 1 hour to fill 6 soda pop cans with pure sweat!

BODY ODOR

Besides sweating more in puberty, your sweat takes on new smells, especially around your armpits, genitals, and feet. You may not be the first one to notice your new odors, but the people around you might! Body odor (BO) can be powerful in a not-so-good way. Some people say it smells like onions. Some people say it smells like a skunk. However it smells, it can be strong. Body odors are another change caused by those circulating hormones that start the whole puberty adventure.

So why does your sweat start to stink in puberty?

Before puberty, sweat comes mostly from **eccrine** (EH krin) **sweat glands,** a type of sweat gland that pushes out mostly water to help with cooling. This type of sweat doesn't really have an odor. Eccrine sweat glands are everywhere (except your lips, ears, and nipples), and they produce clear, watery sweat that is triggered when you are hot to help cool you down.

During puberty, another type of sweat gland, called **apocrine** (AY poh krin) **glands,** start working. Apocrine glands are mostly in your armpits, feet, palms, and around your genitals. They put out an oily yellowish substance along with sweat, so those areas become oilier. And here's the main reason for the new smells: the bacteria that live on your skin (yes, bacteria live on everyone's skin) really think those oils are yummy. As they eat and digest those oils, they release (yes, through little bacteria farts) those stronger odors. During puberty, your apocrine glands are at work all the time, but they work even harder when you're active or exercising or when you're stressed or nervous. That means stress literally stinks! Amazing.

FUN FACT:

Speaking of stink . . . do you think you fart more in puberty? The answer is NO, but most people fart 12 to 25 times a day. That's more than 200,000 farts in a lifetime.

UNSTINKING

So, bacteria digest your body oils and they fart BO. Does that sound gross? There's nothing gross about your body, but most people don't want to smell like BO. The good news is that BO is pretty easy to handle. How do you do that?

Was your first thought deodorant?

Not so fast. There's something else you have to do first!

Wash With Soap!

Once you hit puberty, it's important to wash with soap and water often. Soap is important for washing away the bacteria and the sticky, oily stuff that carries the odor and can stick to your skin and clothes.

When you bathe or shower, you can't just stand under the shower and sing or sit and play in a tub full of water. You actually have to use soap to wash your armpits and your outside private parts where there may already be new hair and where all those new glands are hard at work secreting oils.

Here's why soap matters so much now: those new oils hold all the odors. Have you ever been helping in the kitchen and gotten grease or oil on your hands? Did you rinse it off with just water? Nope. You had to use soap, didn't you? That's why soap is so important for getting rid of smells. All the body odors are attached to the oils on your skin. Water won't take away the smelly oils, but soap will!

It's Wise to Deodorize

After you wash with soap and your pits are dry, *then* comes deodorant. Deodorant is recommended for your armpits but not around your private parts. We talk about keeping your private area clean later on in this chapter.

In terms of deodorant, you have tons of options to choose from. Have you seen the deodorant aisle at your local stores? It can be overwhelming. Most deodorant comes with a built-in antiperspirant too, which helps you sweat less. The deodorant deodorizes you. The antiperspirant stops or decreases the sweat.

Most deodorants have a scent or nice smell to them. Some are fruity or flowery, and some are spicy or sporty. Some smell like cucumbers or rain (What does rain smell like?). Choose whatever smell you like! A lot of the companies that sell deodorants package them to look like some are "feminine" and some are "masculine." How they look totally doesn't matter. Just pick the smell you want because they all work in a similar way, except they just have different smells and labels. Just in case you get overwhelmed or don't even want a fake scent, there are also some without any scent. They are labeled "unscented" or "fragrance-free."

When you shop for deodorant, you might also see body sprays nearby. Body sprays, perfume, and cologne can help cover smells, but they won't stop them! They just put fancy smells on top of stinky smells, and the mixture may be unpleasant. Besides that, too much body spray can keep others away because the sprays can have very strong scents, and they may not smell as great as you think they do.

Unstinking Quickly

If you're at school or away from home and your BO is bothering you, the best way to unstink quickly is to wipe off your armpits with a wet paper towel or moist wipe, let them dry, and then reapply deodorant to dry skin. If you try putting more deodorant over your stink, it won't work very

well. For this reason, some kids like to keep deodorant and moist wipes in their backpack or locker.

THE PITS

Maybe you have the odors under control, but the amount of sweat is giving you wet spots in the armpits of your shirts. Those are called *pit stains.* If they're a problem for you, you can decrease the sweat by using your deodorant with antiperspirant at night after you shower—with soap—and dry your pits completely. That gives the antiperspirant more time to work overnight, and the next day, your pits will be drier.

If that still doesn't take care of the problem, there are clinical-strength deodorants/ antiperspirants with more of the chemical that stops the sweating. Most importantly, if you've tried these things and your sweating still bothers you, definitely talk with your doctor about other ways to help.

The other thing you can do to avoid pit stains is to wear shirts made of fabrics that are "wicking" or "quick dry." Cotton shirts show pit stains and stay wet longer, so avoid those. You can also wear black or dark-colored shirts because pit stains won't show up as well on those colors.

THOSE PRIVATE PARTS

We mentioned that the newly active sweat glands (apocrine glands) are also in your **groin,** which is the area around your private parts where your upper thighs meet your body. It's also an area where new hair may sprout over time. Hair holds odors, so anywhere there's hair, there's likely to be an odor.

There are definitely sweaty odors that happen around your genitals too. That means you should also wash around those areas with soap and water as part of your clean routine. But before you lather up, there are areas within your private parts that can be extra sensitive to soaps or fragrances.

If you have a penis, you should avoid getting soap in the urethra. If you are uncircumcised, you don't want soap under the foreskin either—just water.

But definitely soap up around the base of your penis and your scrotum, and don't miss the area behind your scrotum and your anus!

If you have a vulva, we like to say, "soap on the hair, and just water in there." That means you can soap up the areas with hair, including your groin, mons, labia majora (outer labia), and anus. After you rinse that soapy water off, you can spread the labia majora to wash the creases and folds of the labia minora (inner labia) with just water. Make sure to get any dried discharge out of the creases and folds because that can be a cause of odor. Remember, your vagina cleans itself, so nothing goes in there!

FOOT FUNK

There's one more place that puts out some funky smells around puberty time. Yep, your feet can create some major stink.

Stinky feet are just another part of puberty, and they stink more because of those apocrine glands pumping out oily sweat as a feast for all the bacteria on your feet and in your shoes. There are several things you can do to keep your feet fresh.

- **Soap up!** There's no reason to put deodorant on your feet, but you should be sure to wash them with soap and water every day. You can't count shampoo running over your feet as "washing" them. Rub them with soapy water, including between your toes.
- **Wear clean socks.** Wear cotton or wool socks or footies with any shoes that have closed toes. Make sure they are clean; no turning socks inside out or wearing them for days in a row!
- **Switch up your shoes.** Don't wear the same pair of shoes every single day. Sneakers seem to be the worst, but any shoes can stink. Shoes need some time to air out and let the sweat dry. Giving your favorite pair a day off will pay off!
- **Moisture, begone.** Sprinkle baking soda or baby powder into your shoes to help absorb the moisture your socks don't absorb. And when that's still not doing the trick, a lot of shoes can be tossed into the washing machine to get rid of the bacteria. Just make sure to let them dry completely before wearing them again!

WHAT'S YOUR CLEAN ROUTINE?

As you go through puberty, you'll figure out your favorite ways to manage odors and feel clean and fresh. Once you figure out what works for you, it becomes easy when you have a clean routine! You may do some things every

day (like wear deodorant) and other things less often (like wash your hair). Everyone has their own unique body, so your routine may not be exactly like the routines of your friends.

Taking care of your changing body takes some time to figure out. You may need to try different products, different tricks, and different routines before you find what works best for you and your body. Be patient, and don't be afraid to ask for help if what you're doing isn't working. As you continue to grow, you may need to change the way you take care of yourself. But just make sure you do your best to take good care of you!

Don't you feel fresher already? In the next chapter, you'll meet Kimi, who's learning how to take care of her skin!

CHAPTER 6

THE SKIN YOU'RE IN

KIMI

Ever since the band performance with the stinky bus, I've been showering every day and wearing plenty of deodorant. It's fun to pick out different soaps and deodorant scents to try, and Mom even showed me a few videos online where people recommend the products they like to use. Now she's letting me show a few of the videos to my friends while we cool down after being out in the hot sun.

"So, she's saying that she washes her face twice a day?" Maria asks, pointing to the woman on the computer screen. We're sitting in a circle on the floor, eating Popsicles while we watch.

I nod. "That's what she recommends. But I tried that and it made my skin too dry, so now I only wash my skin at night."

"I wash my face twice a day, and I still get pimples," Jack says. "If it's a really big pimple, I cover it with a little face makeup my mom gave me. Like she does." He points his orange Creamsicle at the screen, where the woman has moved on to showing how to apply concealer with a brush or with your finger.

"I always wear concealer under my eyes," says Damien. "It helps my eye shadow show up better." Damien blinks, showing the washes of purple and pink glitter across his eyelids. He loves expressing himself with makeup, using his face like a canvas for beautiful art.

"I'm not really into using makeup, even if I have a pimple," says Maria, licking her Fudgsicle. "I just stick to my Chapstick. And sunscreen, especially when I'm playing soccer."

"I love using mascara and blush for special occasions," I say. "Speaking of special occasions—Damien, will you do my eye shadow for Halloween? I want to have something green and witchy."

Damien's eyes light up. "Yes! I have the best colors for that."

"Oh, can you help me too?" asks Jack. "I want to be a zombie."

"Sure!" says Damien. "We can do dark colors all around your eyes. I have a great makeup remover I can show you how to use too, because sometimes it can be hard to take off the dark colors. And it helps keep the makeup from clogging your pores."

"That would be great," says Jack. "If I still have zombie eyes on my face the next morning, I'll probably give myself a Halloween scare in the mirror."

I finish the last of my Sour Pop and then stick out my colorful tongue. "Scary like this?"

Jack covers his eyes with his hands, pretending to be terrified.

"What are you going to be for Halloween, Maria?" Damien asks.

"I'm going to be an astronaut," she says. "So no makeup for me. With my helmet on, you won't even know what my face looks like."

"Can I borrow that helmet the next time I get a pimple?" Jack asks.

I laugh. "We should make a video sharing our new beauty tip. Have a pimple? Don't bother to wash your face—just become an astronaut!"

Maria pats Jack on the shoulder. "We always want to see your face, Jack. Pimples and all."

"Yeah, everybody gets pimples," I say. "Imagine if the whole world was wearing astronaut helmets!"

"I'd miss seeing your faces," Jack admits.

Damien points at Maria. "And we'll miss *your* face on Halloween. So you can only wear that helmet for a night!"

"Just one night," Maria says grinning, "I promise."

Along with sprouting new hair, puberty may bring oily skin and pimples, also known as zits or acne. Gee, thanks. And guess what makes your skin get oily? You got it: testosterone. Remember, EVERY body has at least a little testosterone. It's crazy how one hormone can bring on all the hair, oils, and body odor, but it does!

Remember how there's a purpose for your pubic hair (see Chapter 4)? There's also a purpose for the oil on your skin. Oils protect our skin by keeping it soft. Oils also help keep moisture in our bodies and bacteria out. But in puberty, all the new testosterone can make the oil glands get a little overexcited, and they can release more oil than your skin needs. The extra oil can lead to **acne,** which means blackheads and pimples—or zits. Zits are the pits, right?!

FUN FACT: Eight out of 10 kids have some type of acne. It's the most common skin problem in the United States.

Acne can start as young as 7 years old, but it's more common during your big growth spurt. Most people think of acne as something that happens on the face and neck, but it can also show up on the chest and back. What do you call acne on the back? Bacne! Get it? Back + acne!

WHAT IS ACNE?

As testosterone causes the oil glands in your skin to make more oil, the oil glands connect to your pores, which are very, very tiny openings in your skin (you can see them if you look closely).

The oil and cells that line your pores stick together and make a clump or plug that blocks the pore. These plugs are blackheads, and bacteria love to hang out and grow in them. All that bacteria can cause tiny infections that lead to swelling and redness and maybe even pus . . . then a pimple is born!

So acne is *not* caused by dirt, but dirt can make it worse. Even the squeakiest clean skin can have acne. Your genes and ancestors also have a lot to do with the type and amount of acne you get. If your biological parents or family members had acne, you're more likely to have it too.

ACNE DOS AND DON'TS

If you get pimples, there are some things you can do to help, and there are some things you can do that will make them even worse!

Here's the list of things you should NOT do!

- **Picking.** Don't pick! In fact, pinching, picking, and popping your pimples can cause them to become bigger, take longer to heal, or form scars. So no PPPP (pimple pinching, popping, or picking)!

- **Scrubbing.** Scrubbing too hard with a rough cloth or gritty soaps or exfoliators can be harsh on the skin and make acne worse by irritating pores. Always wash with a soft cloth or your clean hands.
- **Covering.** Some people use makeup to cover pimples. Makeup may clog pores even more and make acne worse. If you want to use a cover-up, make sure the package has the words "oil-free," "noncomedogenic," or "won't clog pores."
- **Touching.** When you touch your face with your hands, it spreads more oils and bacteria, which can make acne worse. Anything that touches your face can do the same. Headbands, helmets, or chin

straps can all block pores and worsen acne. If you wear things that rub your face, make sure to wash your face with soap and water afterward.

- **Stressing.** Things that stress your mind or body (like exams, lots of worries, or lack of sleep) can make things worse on your face, back, and chest because stress releases more hormones. Finding healthy ways to manage your stress can help!

Here's the list of things you SHOULD do to make acne better!

- **Washing.** Washing your face twice a day with a mild cleanser (or acne wash) and warm water will do the trick unless you have those zit genes. Remember not to scrub hard. Your hands or a soft washcloth is best.

- **Eating right.** Eating a balanced diet is good for your skin. That means getting plenty of fruits and vegetables and avoiding too many sugary or greasy foods. Believe it or not, chocolate, sweets, and french fries don't really make acne worse (just make sure you choose healthier foods, too).

- **Exercising.** Regular exercise will increase the blood flow to your skin to give it a healthy glow. The increased blood flow also helps remove the bacteria and germs that make acne worse. Just remember that after exercising, it helps to wash the sweat and dirt off your face and other areas that have acne.

- **Removing products.** Try to keep hair products like gel, mousse, oils, or spray off your face and hairline. These products can be oily, and they can block pores.
- **Drinking water.** Drinking plenty of water helps keep the skin clear by improving blood circulation and clearing away the bacteria and germs.

If these simple steps aren't controlling your acne, and your acne bothers you, talk with your parent or another caregiver to see whether you can use some stronger products from the pharmacy or from your doctor. There are a lot of acne washes, creams, and gels available. Find an adult to help you choose a mild product with benzoyl peroxide or salicylic acid (those are the main ingredients in acne treatments). Both of these can help make acne better if you use them carefully. Start with a milder strength, and read the labels so you are using them correctly. If you start with a higher strength or use too much, it can cause your skin to get very dry and red and even peel.

FUN FACT: Washing your face too much can actually make your acne worse by irritating or drying out your skin, which makes more oil. Overdoing it with acne treatments can have the same effect. So stick to a morning and night regimen— cleanse, medicate, and moisturize.

If you decide to use acne products, it's also an important time to add an oil-free lotion. That seems wrong, but here's why it matters. Acne products dry out your skin. When your skin feels dry, it makes more oil, which can worsen acne. Instead, adding the oil-free lotion (also called a *moisturizer*) will stop your skin from feeling dry, and it won't make extra oil. Ta-da!

Whatever steps you take, be patient. It takes about 6 weeks before you'll see the results of a new product or skin care treatment. That means you have to do it every day for 6 weeks! If being patient still doesn't do the trick, you may need to see your doctor. There are lots of other treatments your doctor can recommend to help you.

The menstrual cycle and periods (we explain both of those in Chapter 8) can also worsen acne at certain times because of the added hormones in the body.

Acne can be embarrassing and really frustrating. There may be times when you feel like your acne is so bad that no one wants to hang out with you or that you don't even want to go to school. If you ever feel like this, you are not alone. What's important is to let your parent, another adult you are close with, a counselor, or your doctor know that you feel like this, so you can get help. There are plenty of ways to make your acne better and help you feel better about yourself.

DAILY ROUTINES BECOME . . . ROUTINE

Taking care of your changing body takes some time to figure out. You may need to experiment with different products, different tricks, and different routines before you find what works best for you and your body. Be patient, and don't be afraid to ask for help if what you're doing isn't working.

For now, your day may start like this: brush your teeth, wash your face, get dressed, put on your deodorant, fix your hair, and make your bed. As you get older, you may want to add other steps, like shaving, taking a morning shower, applying acne cream, using makeup, and maybe even putting gel or other products into your hair.

As you go through puberty, you will find that doing the same daily routine makes it easier to take care of your amazing body.

MORNING CHECKLIST
- ☑ BRUSH TEETH
- ☑ WASH FACE
- ☑ GET DRESSED
- ☑ DEODORANT
- ☑ STYLE HAIR
- ☑ MAKE BED

So many changes! In the next chapter, Stephanie is dealing with her chest starting to grow!

CHAPTER 7

BREASTS AND CHESTS

STEPHANIE

I knock on Abigail's door. Through it, I can hear the muffled sound of my older sister talking with someone on the phone.

"OK. Bye, Khalil," she says. Khalil is her boyfriend, who she met at an event where they both spoke about being athletes with Down syndrome. Abigail is only home from college for the weekend, but I know she misses him.

"Come in!" Abigail calls.

I open the door and find her sitting on the bed, with her suitcase half unpacked on the floor.

"What's up?" Abigail asks.

"Hey." I walk in and she scoots over on the bed, making room for me to sit next to her. I cross my arms over my chest, feel a little twinge of discomfort, and then uncross my arms. I take a breath.

"When did you start wearing a bra?" I ask her. "I think I might need to start wearing one soon."

Abigail's face lights up. "That's so exciting!" She thinks for a second. "Um, I think I was the same age as you when I started wearing them. Mom took me bra shopping at the mall, and we bought a bunch of different kinds."

I get an idea. "Do you still have any of those? That I could wear now?"

"Of course!" Abigail stands up and walks over to dig through her closet. When she emerges, she's holding a small basket filled with bras and camis of different sizes and shapes.

"I don't wear any of these anymore. Take whatever you want," she says.

"Wow! Thanks, Abby," I say, starting to pull things out of the basket. Then there's another knock on the door.

"Come in!" Abigail and I say at the same time.

"Everything OK in here?" Mom asks, poking her head through the door. She sees the bras in my hands and smiles. "Do you need any help picking something out? Or I can leave you two to it, if you want some privacy."

I look between the different pieces of fabric, having no idea where to start.

"I could use your help too," I say. "My chest has been hurting when I dance, and I feel like my . . . my . . ."

"Breasts?" Mom offers with a smile.

I nod. "They look pointy in my leotards, not like normal breasts."

Mom steps into the room. "The pointy look you're talking about is a normal stage as your breasts first start to grow. Abigail had the same thing too, when she first started wearing bras." I look at Abigail, and she nods.

"Yeah, I remember it hurting when I was playing sports," Abigail says.

Mom nods. "Your breasts can definitely be sore as they grow. A bra can give you some support, which should help, especially when you're in dance class."

I nod and then look down at all the bras in the basket.

"I also feel like one side is definitely bigger than the other," I tell them. "Is that normal? Is there a certain bra I should wear for that?"

"That's very normal," Mom says. "They will even out a bit as they grow, but many, many people have breasts that are 2 different sizes. Any of these bras should work for you, but we can go shopping for new ones too, to see what you like best."

The door pushes open, this time with no knock. Champ comes bounding into the room, wagging his tail and sniffing at all the bras. We laugh.

"Good boy, Champ!" Abigail exclaims. "He's getting so big!"

"Everyone around here is growing up!" Mom says and puts an arm around me. I hug her back, and Abigail joins in, with Champ jumping up to also join us.

You probably already know what breasts are and what can happen to them in puberty, but there are some details a lot of people don't know. We want you to not only understand what to expect as your own body changes but also understand what your friends may experience.

BUDDING BREASTS

Let's go back to estrogen. Remember how we mentioned that your brain sends out hormones to tell your body when to start puberty (see Chapter 1)? The first hormone for EVERY body is usually the growth hormone that sends a message to the feet and hands, telling them to grow, right? If you are like most girls or some nonbinary or transgender kids, like Oliver, you have ovaries, which also help puberty start by making estrogen. The very first thing the estrogen usually does is telling the breasts that it's time to start growing.

Estrogen does other things besides working on breasts; however, breast growth is the first visible sign of puberty. Each breast starts off with a small hard knot under the areola and nipple. This knot is called a **breast bud,** and it's usually about the size and shape of a blueberry. Normally, breast buds show up anytime from the age of 8 through 12, but the average age is around 10.

Most of the time, one breast buds first, so being lopsided is very common. The other breast usually buds within 3 to 6 months and eventually catches up. Even on the same person, each breast can be a slightly different size. That difference is totally normal!

During all this early growing, it's also normal for breasts, particularly the buds (including the areolae and nipples), to be tender or to hurt if they're touched or bumped. If you have soreness or tenderness, it will usually go away after a few months, but it might return from time to time as your breasts continue to grow.

A knot in the breast can be scary because for grown-ups, it is sometimes a sign of breast cancer. For kids, that's not the case. A knot under the areola around puberty is a breast bud and is totally normal, but if you're ever concerned about anything on your breast or chest, make sure to check with your doctor.

If you haven't seen any breast buds by the age of 13, you should see your doctor for a checkup. Most of the time, late puberty is nothing to worry about, but sometimes a medical problem can stop puberty from happening at the usual time. Your doctor can figure that out and provide treatment, if needed.

FUN FACT:
Even in the adult breast, one side is slightly larger than the other. Most commonly, it's the left side that is larger.

BOY "BOOBS"

Estrogen is made by ovaries at the beginning of puberty, but even boys and kids like Kimi, who make mostly testosterone during puberty, still have some estrogen in their bodies. That's right. They don't have ovaries that make estrogen, but a little bit of the testosterone made by their testes gets turned into estrogen. It's  complicated science, but that small amount of estrogen is enough to make breasts grow a little. In fact, about half of all boys and kids like Kimi will naturally have a little breast growth during puberty. It's called **gynecomastia** (guy nuh koh MAST ee ya), and it's totally normal and common. It can make the nipples and areolae get larger and darker, and one or both breasts may start to stick up or even hurt a little. Some kids worry a lot about it, but knowing that it goes away as you move further along in puberty helps.

HOW BREASTS GROW

Remember how we mentioned that doctors describe pubic hair growth from stages 1 to 5 (see Chapter 4)? We do the same thing for breast growth because it helps us know whether someone is growing like they should, and it helps us predict when they can expect other puberty changes to happen.

Let's look at the following breast development stages. If your body makes mainly estrogen, you can find the stage you are in right now. If you don't expect to be growing breasts, you can still learn what happens and understand what some of your friends might experience.

- **Stage 1:** There is no breast growth at all. Nothing has started. Nada. Zero. Nothing. This is the way EVERY body looks before puberty starts.
- **Stage 2:** This stage begins as soon as there is a breast bud. Sometimes you can feel the bud before you even see it. It may feel like a hard knot under the areola and nipple. And remember, it's common for it to be tender. Although one side usually buds at a time, both breasts should bud before you move into stage 3.
- **Stage 3:** After the breasts bud and the areolae look larger and darker in color, there will be a small fatty mound of breast tissue that forms on the chest and pushes the nipples and areolae farther out. Sometimes the breasts look a little pointy, or sometimes they may look like a rounded mound.
- **Stage 4:** This stage is sometimes hard to notice, but it's when the nipple and areola stick farther off the breast mound. It can look like there are 2 lumps making up each breast. Some kids never really notice this stage, but others may not like the way their breasts look during this stage.

FUN FACT: Breasts are made of glands, ducts, and blood vessels, not just fat.

- **Stage 5:** This is the final stage, when the breasts are grown and shaped like an adult's breasts (but remember that breasts come in many different sizes and shapes). Most people's breasts are not completely finished growing until they are 17 or 18 years old, so this stage can last for several years.

BIG OR SMALL

A lot of people worry about their breast size because breasts can get a lot of attention. Sometimes, people say mean or disrespectful things about other people's breasts. There may be teasing about someone who is flat chested or teasing about someone who has large breasts. Teasing about breasts is immature and wrong. Besides teasing, sometimes people just get silly when talking about breasts.

The truth is, for breasts that grow from a lot of estrogen, they come in all different shapes and sizes. But no matter what size breasts are, they can all make breast milk.

If you are growing breasts, you may feel like yours are too big or too small. Often, people with big breasts wish theirs were smaller. And people with small breasts wish they had bigger ones. This thinking is kind of like how people with curly hair want straight hair, and those with straight hair wish they had curls. Sometimes we just think that life would be better, easier, or more fun if we had something different. Guess what? Most of the time, this thinking is just plain wrong.

FUN FACT:
A baby can live and grow on nothing but breast milk for the first 6 months after they are born.

BREAST Q&A

We hear a lot of questions from kids about breasts, and you might wonder about the same things. Here are some of those questions and our answers.

Q: If I develop breasts earlier than my friends, does that mean my breasts will be bigger than theirs when I'm grown?

A: Not at all, your breast size is mostly determined by your **genetics** (what you inherit through your biological parents). Some kids who develop early may end up with smaller breasts, and some who develop later may have bigger ones. Besides genetics, your breast size can be affected by your weight. If you gain extra weight, you'll gain weight in your breasts, as well as your belly, legs, and everywhere else. If you lose weight, you may also find that your breast size decreases.

Q: If my mom has small breasts, does that mean I will too?

A: Maybe, maybe not. Again, the answer depends on your genetics. It doesn't matter whether you have a mom and dad, 2 moms, 2 dads, or one parent, your genetics come from the 2 people who provided the egg and the sperm

that made you. When it comes to your breast size, you still inherit some of your size and shape from your biological father and his ancestors. So your breasts may be more like your aunts' or grandmother's on your biological father's side than like your biological mom's. Every person is a new mixture of traits that makes them unique.

Q: Can I make my breasts grow more with pills or special exercises?

A: Nope, no matter what you see on the internet or TV, there are no pills or exercises that make you grow more breast tissue. Sometimes the muscles under the breasts may get bigger with *a lot* of exercise, but they don't change your breast size. Remember, having breasts is not about how they look; it's about what they do!

FUN FACT:

Humans are the only mammals who grow permanent breasts. Other mammals grow breasts only when they are pregnant or breastfeeding, but then they go away.

Q: I don't want my breasts to grow. Can I do anything to keep them small?

A: For some kids, developing breasts feels really wrong. Sometimes this happens when kids start growing breasts a lot sooner than their friends. Other times this happens if kids don't feel like they should ever grow breasts. If you are worried that developing breasts feels really wrong for you, make sure to talk with your doctor about that.

Q: When my breasts start to grow, does that mean I'll start my period soon?

A: We cover periods in Chapter 8, but the short answer is no. When your breasts start to grow, that signals the beginning of puberty. It takes several years to move all the way through puberty. For most people, periods start to happen about 2 to 3 years after breasts bud.

Q: Do I *have* to wear a bra?

A: Nobody has to wear a bra, but if your breasts are growing, especially if they are tender or sore, you may want to wear one for comfort. Some kids are embarrassed about wearing a bra because they don't want anyone to know that they're developing. Remember that a lot of your classmates may be developing at the same time, so you're not alone! Developing breasts might feel a little embarrassing when it first starts, but before long, you'll get used to it!

Q: When is it time to wear a bra?

A: There is no age or stage that makes it the right time to wear a bra. The timing is up to you! If you think you should, you might want to get advice from someone else you know and trust who also wears a bra.

Some kids start wearing a bra because their friends are wearing a bra. Some wear one because it's more comfortable for their tender breasts. There is no right or wrong time, but there are some common reasons why some kids decide to start wearing a bra. You might want to wear a bra if you notice that your breasts are . . .

- Beginning to show through your clothes
- Starting to jiggle when you walk
- Feeling heavy
- Feeling sore

Because tender breasts can hurt more when they move around, a bra can hold your breasts snug to your body, so there's less movement. Bras can also keep your growing breasts more private. In Chapter 10, you can learn more about bras and choosing one that works for your body!

Isn't it amazing how EVERY body has similarities and differences, even when it comes to breasts and chests? But then, even when bodies are alike, they have a lot of differences. And when bodies are different, they still have a lot in common!

CHAPTER 8

ALL ABOUT PERIODS, PERIOD

MARIA

'm in art class, getting lost in the swirls of bright pink, orange, and purple as I paint the sunset across my canvas.

Then I feel another wave of achiness in my back. I stop painting, trying to stretch and straighten it. My stomach has been hurting all day. I had an empanada for lunch. It tasted amazing, but maybe there was something wrong with it.

Finally, I set down my paintbrush and get a bathroom pass from Ms Chen. Shreya looks at me with her eyebrows raised as I leave the room, so I give her the best smile I can manage. Walking makes me feel a little better, and before I know it, I'm in a bathroom stall, alone.

But as soon as I pull down my pants, I realize what's going on.

I've started my period, for the very first time!

My heart races as I check my pants for signs of blood leaking through. Did anyone see? Could everyone tell? I remember the way Ms Chen met my eyes when she gave me the bathroom pass, as well as Shreya's look as I walked out. They could definitely tell. My face flushes with embarrassment. How can I go back in there now?

"Maria?" Shreya's voice comes from outside the stall. "Are you OK?"

She knows!

"Um, I'm fine," I say. "What are you doing here?"

"Ms Chen sent me to check on you. She thought you might be getting sick in here and might need me to get the nurse."

Getting sick?

"Actually, I . . . uh . . . ," I begin. I stare at the cracks of light around the stall door and take a deep breath. "I've started my period, for the very first time."

"No way! That's so exciting!" Shreya exclaims.

"It is?"

"Yeah!" I hear her feet jumping up and down on the tiles. But then they stop. "Oh, do you need a pad? Or a tampon?"

"I, uh—"

"Hang on, I'll be just a second," Shreya says, and I hear her hurry out of the bathroom. Before I know it, she's back.

"Here," Shreya says. She passes me a sparkly little bag under the stall door. I unzip it to find an array of wrapped items, some flat and some shaped like tubes.

"What should I use?"

"You might want to try a pad first," Shreya says. "That's what I did, anyway. Those are the flat blue ones. You just peel off the back and put the sticky part on the inside of your underwear, like a sticker. And take an extra in case you want to change into a fresh one later."

I follow her instructions, surprised by how easy it is to put on. When I'm dressed again, I stick an extra pad in my pocket and exit the stall to wash my hands.

"I'm so glad you already had your period," I tell Shreya. "I thought I was the first one."

Shreya smiles at me in the mirror. "I've had it a few times now. But my sister didn't start hers until she was years older than we are. Everyone's different, I guess."

I dry my hands on a paper towel and hand her back her bag.

"I'm scared to go back in there," I confess. "I feel like it's written all over me that I just got my period."

"The only thing written all over you is what a great artist you are!" Shreya says, pointing at the different colors of paint  streaked across my arms. I laugh, and we walk back to art class together.

That night, my mom gives me pads of my own. I put a few into a small polka-dotted bag and tuck it into my backpack. One day, maybe I'll be able to hand it to someone else, just like Shreya did for me.

You have probably already heard a little something about periods. And we're not talking about the dot that ends a sentence. The period that happens in puberty is also called **menstruation** or the **menstrual period.** It's a very normal and healthy thing that happens for anyone with a uterus and a vagina. Periods start a couple of years into puberty and happen about once a month for many years. Getting a period is a pretty big deal during puberty, and there's a lot to know about them.

FUN FACT:
Before 1985, the word *period* had never been said on American TV.

THE BEGINNING

When a period starts, there is bloody fluid that trickles out of the vagina for about 3 to 7 days. That may sound scary, but it is actually an amazing and pretty miraculous event! When someone starts having periods, it's a sign their body is growing and developing like it should.

It's no secret: the whole reason people have periods is so they can have babies one day, if they want to. But having a period won't make a baby. It takes a lot more than that to make a baby. It takes a male body *and* a female body. That's another big topic. For now, let's stick with puberty and periods.

Periods start in the preteen or teen years because the uterus needs time to mature and become ready. Hormones start the process by sending a message to the uterus and ovaries. The ovaries release an egg about each month. The uterus responds by turning the endometrium, the inside layer of the uterus, into a thick, cozy "bed" where a baby could grow. The endometrium gathers blood, nutrients, and fluffy tissue to make it thick and lush. Why?

If you think about what humans need to survive, this process makes sense. All people need shelter and safety, food and water, and oxygen. Believe it or not, the uterus and endometrium provide exactly this type of environment for a growing baby. The uterus provides the shelter and safe place to grow. The endometrium is lined with nutrients and fluids. And there is blood that brings oxygen to the baby. What a cool little habitat.

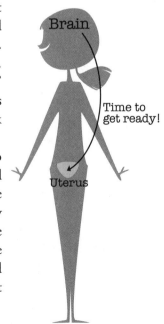

Brain

Time to get ready!

Uterus

IT'S A CYCLE

Now back to the bed. If there's no baby (which is most of the time), the uterus clears out the endometrium to build a new, fresh lining. It's sort of like if the uterus says, "Oh well, no baby here! It's time to change the sheets." It releases, or sheds, the lining of the endometrium, which passes through the cervix and out of the vagina as bloody fluid. That's what people call a **period** or **menstrual flow.**

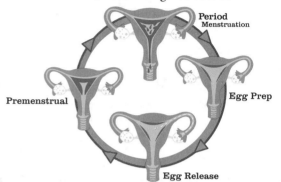

The whole period contains less than a couple of tablespoons of actual blood. But it seems like more because of the other fluids and tissue that come out with it. After shedding the endometrium lining, the uterus starts over by rebuilding the endometrium bed with a fresh lining. This happens about once every month. That's why periods are called a *cycle*, or more specifically, the **menstrual cycle.** As soon as one period begins, the brain sends out hormones that signal the uterus to start preparing the endometrium again in a new cycle.

WHEN WILL MY PERIOD START?

Most people with a uterus and vagina will eventually get a period. If you expect to have periods, wouldn't it be nice to get a phone call or a text message to tell you when one will arrive? Unfortunately, that doesn't happen. No phone call, no text, no DM . . . nothing. There is no way to predict exactly when all this great stuff will happen, but you can use a few clues to guide you.

Remember that EVERY body develops on their own time schedule, so even though you and your friend may start to develop at the same time, you might start to have your periods many months, or even years, apart.

Look for the following events or times to help you know when you might be close to getting your first period:

NEW MESSAGE:
TOMORROW
IS THE
DAY!

- 1½ to 3 years after your breasts bud
- After a growth spurt of several inches over 3 to 6 months
- When your breasts are in or near stage 4 (See Chapter 7.)
- When your pubic hair reaches stage 3 or 4 (See Chapter 4.)

If you have a health condition or if you are very athletic or thin, your period may start later. If you haven't started your period by the age of 15, visit your doctor for a checkup to make sure everything is OK. There are lots of reasons this might happen, and your doctor is the best person to help you.

THE FIRST PERIOD

The very first period is called **menarche** (MEN are kee). You might think you will feel it the second it starts, but sometimes you don't even know a period has started until you see it. That's because you've already been having vaginal discharge, which can make you feel a little wet or damp in your underwear. The moment your period starts may not feel any different because a period usually starts with just a little bloody fluid. Periods won't ever shoot out or pour out. They trickle.

Also, a period may not look exactly like fresh blood. Because it's made of blood, tissue, and other fluids, it can look thicker and it can be pink to brown to maroon and even blackish. All those colors are totally normal!

Remember, most periods last about 3 to 7 days. In the first day or two, it is typical to have a heavier flow. The flow is usually lighter toward the end of a period. If every period lasts longer than 7 days, or if any period lasts longer than 2 weeks, it's important to check in with your doctor.

Some people may have dark clumps of blood, called *clots*. Clots are dark, gooey globs that happen anytime blood stays in one place for a while, like your vagina. You are most likely to see clots in the morning from the menstrual blood that built up in your vagina while you were lying down. If you have clots that are bigger than a quarter throughout the day, let your doctor know. This can be a sign your periods are too heavy.

YOUR MONTHLY VISITOR

After menarche, your second period might start about a month later or might take several months to arrive. It takes your body a while to get used to having periods, and the first 3 periods are the most unpredictable. In general, adults get a period about every month. For young tweens or teens, it's less regular, but after you've had a few periods, one should still come at least every 3 to 6 weeks.

PERIOD PROTECTION

Of course, if you have periods, you will need to figure out what helps you manage your flow. If you don't, blood will leak onto your clothes and bedsheets. There are products that absorb your flow to keep stains off clothes, furniture, and bed linens.

Have you ever seen the aisle at the grocery store or pharmacy that is labeled "feminine hygiene"? It's the aisle with hundreds of brightly colored boxes. Why so many? They all have to do with periods, so we prefer the term **period products** to describe them. There are pads, tampons, menstrual cups, and even period underwear! Every person has different likes and dislikes when it comes to taking care of their menstrual flow, and that's why there are so many period products available. Let's run through all the different types.

Pads

Most young people prefer to use a **pad** with their first period. A pad, also called a **sanitary napkin** (Who came up with that weird name?), is an oval or rectangular cottony piece of material that fits in your underwear and absorbs menstrual blood. Pads are made with a sticky side that holds them in the crotch of underwear. Using one is easy: just unwrap the pad, pull off the paper that covers the adhesive (sticky) strip, and put the pad in your underwear. The sticky side goes against your underwear, *not* against *you*—ouch! As you pull up your underwear, you'll want to make sure the pad is centered under your vagina. If it is too far forward or backward, the bloody fluid might end up in your underwear instead of on the pad.

Pads With "Wings"

Pads with "wings" were invented to help prevent leaking and overflow that may happen when a pad bunches up in the middle. Sometimes a lot of running or other physical activity will make a pad bunch up so the menstrual flow goes over the edge and stains underwear. Wings are extra flaps with their own adhesive strips that wrap around the crotch of underwear. Some people like wings, some don't. Most types of pads come with or without wings. It's all about having choices.

Choosing a Pad

Just like people come in different sizes and shapes, pads come in different sizes and shapes to match your body type as well as your period flow. There are shorter pads for petite people and longer pads for bigger or taller people. And then there are the "minis," the "maxis," the "supers," and the "lights" for differences in flow. How's a person to choose? Trying out different types and sizes can help someone find their favorite. Here is a list of some of the types available.

- **Panty liners.** These are very thin pads that work for very light bleeding, which is common toward the end of a period. Some people also like to use these for the vaginal discharge they have between periods.
- **Light or regular pads.** These pads are a little thicker or more absorbent than a panty liner. They are best for light to normal menstrual flow.
- **Super pads.** Maxi-pads are fluffy and big, and they can feel pretty thick. But they sure come in handy when your period is the heaviest.

- **Overnight pads.** As you can imagine, when you lie down your flow can run in different directions. Overnight pads are longer and bigger to help cover a larger part of your underwear while you sleep. Some people just use a regular pad at night. Some people like overnight pads during the day. Again, there are choices because people have different preferences.
- **Reusable pads.** For the environmentally conscious person, reusable pads are made of cotton or special absorbent fabric, so they can be washed and reused. They are better for the environment because they keep disposable products out of landfills. Most health food or natural food stores carry them, and they are also available through catalogs and online.

Scented or Not?

Besides choosing from all these different shapes and sizes, you'll also choose between deodorized and non-deodorized pads. Deodorized pads have a perfume-like smell to them. When menstrual blood mixes with sweat, it can have an odor. But if you bathe with soap and water daily, especially during your period, you won't need to worry about menstrual odor. There is no smell that anyone would be able to notice. If you feel more comfortable with using deodorized pads, go ahead. But some people develop skin irritations or itching from the perfumes in the pads.

Speaking of odor, the other things you might see in the feminine hygiene aisle are special feminine deodorant sprays. They are made to be sprayed in your groin, but they are not at all necessary. We're not sure who decided that a vulva should smell like a flower, but it really doesn't and it shouldn't. As long as you wash daily, there is no need for these sprays or perfumes. They can actually irritate the sensitive skin of the vulva, so we do not recommend them.

How Long Do Pads Last?

You already know that your period will last 3 to 7 days. Pads last only 3 to 7 *hours* depending on your flow. Your pad will probably never be completely covered in blood, but once the center part gets pretty full, it's time to change it. Also, don't wear the pad so long that it starts to feel soaked or soggy. Pads are made to pull the moisture away from your skin. When your pad starts to feel wet or mushy, you will know that it is time to change it.

So, when your pad is full, do you just pull it off and flush it down the toilet? Please don't! Pads will absolutely clog a toilet or cause it to back up and overflow, which can be embarrassing and not good for the plumbing!

When you are changing a pad, make sure to wrap it in toilet paper or the wrapper from the new pad you are putting on, and place it into the trash can. At home, you should have a trash can near your toilet. You should also get into the habit of emptying your own trash can when it has used pads in it. In time, they will start to smell bad. Have a dog? Take the trash out even more often! It can be really embarrassing to have your dog prancing around with your used pad in their mouth!

At school or out in public, most bathroom stalls have a special small trash container on the stall wall for used pads. Ah, so that's what it's for! You thought it was for used gum, didn't you? Now you know. If there's no bin in the stall, there should always be a trash can somewhere in the bathroom. By cleaning up after yourself, you are showing responsibility. This is one of those growing-up things that show you are taking care of yourself and your body.

Period Underwear

If you're interested in using something that doesn't create as much trash, or if pads just don't sound fun, you can consider period underwear, which is becoming more and more popular with young people. Period underwear is real underwear with a built-in lining that is made of superabsorbent and leakproof fabric. It's washable, so you can reuse it over and over. Having a few pairs can get you through your period, and they can last several years! Some kids use period underwear as a backup for pads or tampons, some prefer it for sleeping, and others use period underwear all the time.

How does it feel? Believe it or not, the fabric feels soft and thin (not like a diaper or a pad)! There are plenty of sizes, styles, absorbencies, and brands to choose from, and most of them are available online.

Time for Tampons?

Most people choose to use pads with their first period. Sometimes, though, a pad just won't do the job you need it to do. Then it may be time to consider tampons.

Have you ever unwrapped a tampon to see how one works? If you have some lying around your house (usually under a bathroom cabinet), give seeing how they work a try. A **tampon** is a small cylinder-shaped cotton tube that actually fits inside the vagina and absorbs the menstrual blood as it

comes out of the cervix. Putting one in may sound painful, but really, if a tampon is put in correctly, it's not even noticeable.

Why on earth would anyone want to use a tampon? Tampons are nice because sometimes, a bulky pad doesn't work. Can you imagine trying to wear a pad to go swimming? (Have you ever seen a soaked swim diaper?) No thanks.

For swimmers, dancers, and gymnasts, tampons are sometimes a necessity. For everyone else, their use just depends on your preference. Some people never want to use a tampon, and other people can't imagine having a period without using tampons. It's all about what a person likes or needs.

What if you are a swimmer, like Shreya, and you start your very first period the day before a huge meet? Do you have to skip the meet? No way, you can use a tampon with your very first period if you want. Your period shouldn't stop you from doing any of the activities you enjoy.

Most people who don't have a big swim meet or another emergency need for a tampon like to try their first tampon after they have had a few periods.

How to Use a Tampon

Tampons are put into the vagina by using something called an *applicator*. An applicator is made of smooth cardboard or plastic and helps the tampon slide into the vagina. If you decide you want to try a tampon, make sure you read the instructions that come with the box. Even then, you may need help from your mom, another trusted person who has used tampons, or maybe even an older sister or friend. Some people do fine by themselves. A mirror can help too.

If you have a vagina, putting something in there may sound scary, but once you learn how to use a tampon, it's easy! First, you need to know the parts of the tampon: the applicator, the tampon, the string, and the plunger—and the grooves for holding all these. Then follow these steps.

1. Find a position that lets you comfortably reach your vagina. You may want to sit on the toilet or squat.
2. Do your best to relax! A few deep breaths help!
3. Unwrap the tampon, and hold it by the gripper grooves with the string hanging down.
4. Find your vaginal opening by using a mirror or your finger.
5. Hold the tampon between your thumb and middle finger as shown:
6. Insert the tampon gently into your vagina, and aim it toward your lower back. That's the normal angle of the vagina.
7. Push it in until your fingers touch your vulva.
8. Push the plunger all the way in (you can push the plunger with your pointer finger on the same hand or use your other hand to help).
9. Pull the applicator out.
10. Your tampon will be in your vagina, and the string will be on the outside. Ta-da!

Tampon Tips

If you have trouble getting the tampon into your vagina, here are some things to try.

- Relax more.
- Use a mirror to see what you are doing.
- Try again when your flow is a little heavier.
- Put a small dab of lubricant (slimy stuff you can buy in the period product aisle) on the very tip of the applicator to help it slide in more smoothly. Don't use petroleum jelly, like Vaseline, or lotion. Use a lubricant that is made to use only in the vagina.
- Try again later.
- Ask for help from someone who has used tampons before.

You'll know whether you have the tampon in correctly by the way it feels. If you can't feel it, it's in right. If it's uncomfortable and makes you want to waddle when you walk, you didn't push it far enough into your vagina. You can use your finger to push it in higher, or you can pull it out, by using the string, and start over with a new tampon.

All tampons have a string on them. To get the tampon out, you just pull slowly but firmly on the string. Don't worry, the string won't break. Even if it did, the vagina is sort of a dead end, so a tampon cannot get lost inside your body.

Should I Practice for the Big Day?

Does all this information make you want to practice for the big day? No way! There's no need to practice, but it's fine to open up a tampon and see what it looks like. You can even dip it in a glass of water to see what happens to it. You should use a tampon only when you are actually having a period! If you're not having your period, there won't be enough fluid in your vagina to wet the tampon. The tampon needs to be wet with your menstrual flow before you take it out. Taking out a dry tampon pulls on the vagina and can hurt.

Choosing the Right Tampon

As you might expect, there are different sizes and shapes of tampons—just like there are of pads. The first time you use one, try a slender or light size. Tampons of this size are thinner and smaller than regular or super tampons. That makes them more comfortable to use until you get better at putting tampons in and taking them out.

The light tampons are for lighter flows. The regular are for normal flows. And the super and super-plus are for really heavy flows. They will all fit into a normal-sized vagina, but it's always easier to start with the smallest ones.

If you use tampons, there is no need for scented tampons (even though you may see them on the shelves in the store). Blood has no odor while it is inside the vagina. With tampons, the blood stays in the vagina on the tampon until you change it. The scented tampons are pretty useless, and the perfumes used in them can cause irritation.

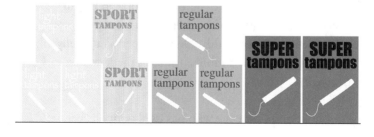

When Should I Change My Tampon?

You can't look at a tampon to see when it is getting full (because it is inside you). Instead, you have to judge by the way it feels, or just change your tampons regularly. When a tampon gets full, the menstrual flow will soak the string and even leak out onto your underwear. For that reason, some people like to wear a panty liner, a light pad, or period underwear along with a tampon until they are more confident with using tampons.

You should never wear a tampon for more than 8 hours, but 4 to 6 hours is best. If you're using the right size for your flow, most tampons will last about only 4 hours. We don't recommend using them at night while you sleep. In your groggy morning routine, you might forget you have one in there and forget to take it out. And if you're getting the sleep you really need, it might be in for more than 8 hours.

Are Tampons Dangerous?

Some people worry about an infection called **toxic shock syndrome (TSS)** that has been linked to incorrect tampon use and can be very serious. Toxic shock syndrome can affect anyone, not just people using tampons; fortunately, it's very rare. You can reduce the chance of TSS by always using the lowest-absorbency tampon that will manage your flow, never wearing one for more than 8 hours, and alternating pads and tampons throughout your period. The symptoms of TSS are a lot like those of the flu: high fever, nausea, vomiting, diarrhea, body aches, and sometimes a rash. If you are ever using a tampon and have these symptoms, it's important to take out the tampon and get medical attention right away.

To Flush or Not to Flush: Tampon Disposal

Like with pads, you'll need to be responsible when you use tampons. When you remove a tampon, it's best to wrap it up and throw it into the trash. There are some tampons and even applicators with packaging that says they can be flushed, but we don't recommend flushing them! Be kind to your plumbing (and keep the plumbers away)!

Menstrual Cups

If you want to use something like a tampon but would like to create less trash or save money, you could consider a menstrual cup. This is a soft, flexible small cup that you fold and insert into your vagina, and it collects the menstrual flow as it comes out of the cervix. Once the cup fills with menstrual flow, you can remove it, empty it, wash it, and reuse it! It's not necessarily the easiest thing to use, especially when you first start your period, but as you become more comfortable with your flow and your vagina, it's another environmentally friendly option that can be used over and over for years.

FUN FACT:

Over a lifetime, a menstruating person who uses pads and tampons will use somewhere between 5,000 and 15,000 total period products.

TIPS FOR PERIOD TROUBLES

Having a period can present some new challenges and even some frustrations for you. The following tips might make things a little easier:

- **While you sleep.** If you're a wild sleeper or have a heavy flow, it can help to place a towel under you at night in case you soak through or spill over your pad. That way, you can wash just the towel instead of all your bedsheets. Another great option for nighttime is to wear period underwear.
- **Stains.** If you get blood on your clothes or sheets (and you probably will), wash them as soon as you can and use cold water and soap. Hot water can make a blood stain harder to get out. A brief washing by hand can get most of the stain out. The rest will usually come out in the laundry.
- **Tough stains!** If you have a large or heavy stain that is tough to get out, a mild chemical called *hydrogen peroxide* (you can buy it at a pharmacy) can help dissolve the blood. Ask a grown-up for help using it because it can change or fade the color of some fabrics. If you have a big mess, ask for help! Don't spray spot removers or use bleach directly on the crotch of your underwear. These are harsh chemicals that can cause a lot of irritation to the skin of your vulva and vagina.

- **No pads.** If you start your period and don't have any period products handy, you can put some toilet paper into your underwear and head to the school nurse's office, to your backpack, or to your best friend for help. Toilet paper won't work for long because it tends to "wander" in your underwear.

- **Leaks.** If your clothing is stained, first ask a friend whether the stain is visible. A lot of period stains look horrible to you, but people behind you can't even see the stain! If it's visible, tie a sweater or jacket around your waist until you can change your clothes. If you worry about leaks, you might consider wearing period underwear along with a pad or tampon. Having that backup protection can help you stop worrying and focus on more important things!

PREDICTING FUTURE PERIODS

Now that you know you'll need products, you can stay prepared by knowing when to expect your next period. The best way to predict future periods is to keep a record of them and watch for a pattern. This is called *tracking your periods,* and you can do it with a calendar, a notebook, or an app (but always check with a parent before downloading any apps). To track your periods, write down the date you start each period. After you have tracked a few periods, you can begin to see a pattern and predict your next period. It's nice to be prepared!

If you count the number of days from the first day of one period to the first day of the next, that is called your **cycle length.** For the first few years after menarche, it is normal for cycle length to be anywhere between 21 and 45 days. If your cycle length is shorter or longer, your doctor will need to know. It's especially important for them to know if your cycle length often lasts more than 45 days or ever lasts more than 90 days, both of which can signal other hormonal or health problems that need attention.

If you have any other concerns about your period (or if you just want to understand your body better), it's a great idea to also keep track of how many days each period lasts, how many period products you use each day, and any other symptoms you have around your period, like headaches or mood changes. If you see a doctor about period problems, the doctor will always want to know the date your last period started and the other details just mentioned. Period tracking helps you understand your body and may help your doctor take better care of you!

DOES IT HURT?

Because periods involve blood, a lot of kids worry that they will be painful. Usually, periods are not painful, but they may be a little uncomfortable. When periods cause cramping in the lower abdomen or pelvis, it's called **menstrual cramps** or just **cramps.** Cramps are most common a little before or right at the beginning of a period. Some people also have cramps or aches in their vulva, upper thighs, or lower back.

Cramps happen because the uterus, which is made of muscle, squeezes to release the endometrial lining that makes up a period. As your uterus squeezes, it can cramp just like any muscle that works hard.

The best way to treat period cramps is to exercise, take a warm bath, or use a heating pad. If none of these help, we recommend taking a medication such as ibuprofen or naproxen. These medications are available at pharmacies or grocery stores without a prescription, but you should take medications only with permission from a parent or another adult you trust. Always be sure to follow the directions on the package. You may see other products that are labeled to treat "premenstrual symptoms," but these have unnecessary ingredients and don't usually work as well.

Finally, if you have cramps that don't get better with medications and are bad enough to stop you from going to school or doing things you enjoy, it's important to talk with your doctor. Periods should never stop you from doing your usual activities, and your doctor can offer other treatments that can help.

PMS (PREMENSTRUAL SYNDROME)

Some people notice changes in their body and emotions before a period starts. That's called **PMS,** which stands for **premenstrual syndrome.** It's caused by the hormones that go up and down as they control the menstrual cycle, especially right before the start of each period. You already know that hormonal changes can make emotions feel bigger. With PMS, some people may feel more emotional or moody before a period, then they're back to feeling normal a day or two after their period starts. But PMS doesn't affect just emotions.

It can also include body symptoms like breast tenderness, acne, diarrhea, headaches, or cramps.

If you have PMS, it can help to know that these changes will go away on their own. Sometimes, just knowing when to expect the symptoms can help you prepare for them, manage them, and know that they are only temporary (that's another reason period tracking is helpful)!

PERIODS ARE PRIVATE BUT NO BIG SECRET

If you get your first period, it's important to tell your mom, your dad, or another adult you trust because you will probably need some help buying or finding period supplies.

You might feel embarrassed, excited, or unsure, but remember that about half of all the people in the world get periods! Even people who don't get periods know about them and can help you.

We hope you are comfortable or become more comfortable with talking about periods. Periods are normal, and you can shout that from the rooftops!

YOU'RE STILL A KID!

Getting your period is a big step toward growing up. But guess what? You're still a kid. Having a period doesn't mean you have to act like an adult. Please don't! Keep doing all your great kid things: dance, play soccer, tumble, run, climb trees, and catch fireflies. Your period shouldn't change any of this fun or slow you down at all. Onward!

CHAPTER 9

TESTOSTERONE ZONE

LESHAUN

Who would like to come up to the board to show us how they solved this problem?" Mr Martinez asks. "Leshaun? How about you?"

I look up from my notebook, with my body frozen at my desk. I had noticed that funny feeling starting a little while ago, so when I look down at my lap, I already know what I will see. I have a boner, and it's sticking up in my pants in a way *everyone* will see if I go up to the board to solve this math problem.

Why did this happen? I was thinking about *math,* about numbers, about solving the problem. I know I got the answer right. But there's no way I can go up to the board in front of everyone now.

I keep my eyes down on my notes, feeling every eye in the class turn toward me.

"I can't answer it," I say. The room is silent for a moment.

"Are you not feeling well, Leshaun?" Mr Martinez asks. I still don't look up at him, but I can hear the concern in his voice. He, and everyone else in this room, knows I've never said I don't know how to solve a math problem. "Do you need to go to the nurse?"

"I'm OK," I say.

Thankfully, he moves on to calling on someone else. Although the boner fades away, I can't help but feel awkward and embarrassed for the rest of the lesson. I'm always the one Mr Martinez can count on to come up and solve the problem. Everyone must know what happened to me. I can barely look anyone in the eye for the rest of the day.

That night, after my brothers and sisters go to their rooms and only my mom is sitting at the kitchen table, I work up the courage to tell her.

"I couldn't go up to the board to solve a problem in math today," I tell her. Mom sets down the papers she's reading. "And it was hard to focus on my notes."

"But you've always loved math, Leshaun," she asks, looking just as worried as Mr Martinez did. "Do you think you need a tutor? Or to talk with Dr Gupta about your trouble focusing?"

I shake my head. "I might need to see Dr Gupta, but not to talk with her about focusing. It's actually because I . . ." I take a breath. "I had a boner, in class. I think something is wrong with me."

Mom shakes her head, smiling a little.

"Nothing is wrong with you," she says. "What you're talking about is completely normal, especially at your age."

I feel a huge weight lift off of my shoulders. "Really?"

"Really," Mom says. "And if it becomes more common in a way that makes you uncomfortable, or you still have trouble focusing at school, we can talk with Dr Gupta. But this probably wasn't your first erection," Mom says. I nod, and she continues. "And it definitely won't be your last. What did you do instead of going up to the board?"

"I stayed at my desk. Mr Martinez asked me if I needed to go to the nurse, but I told him I didn't. Then I kept thinking about math, and it went away pretty quickly."

Mom nods. "It sounds like you did a great job handling it, Leshaun. There's no reason to be embarrassed or worried." She puts a hand on my shoulder. "Do you want to talk with Dad about it tonight? I'm sure he can give you a few tips on how to handle it in the future." She smiles. "And you two math lovers can talk all about that problem you were supposed to solve."

"That would be great," I say, already feeling so much better. "Thanks, Mom."

You've already learned that even a little testosterone will make EVERY body grow new hair, new odors, and new pimples. But what if someone has a LOT of testosterone—like the amount sent out from the testes in puberty?

For most boys, testosterone made during puberty will change their penis, testes, and scrotum and their inside parts involved in sperm making. Testosterone is also the reason for other puberty changes, like deeper voices, mustaches, beards, broader shoulders, and bigger muscles. And just like doctors have stages to describe the growth of breasts and pubic hair, we also have 5 stages to describe how testosterone gradually changes the penis and testes during puberty.

If you have testes making testosterone, there are other body changes that will happen during these stages, and they'll all be pretty amazing! It can make you feel more confident to know what's ahead. Even if your body won't experience these changes, it's still a great time to learn what your friends or family members will go through.

PUBERTY STAGES

Stage 1: Prepuberty

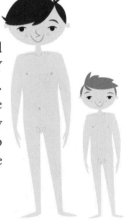

Stage 1 is really prepuberty. Just like the stages for breast and pubic hair growth, there is no stage 0. That means EVERY body is in stage 1 before the hormones of puberty kick in. If you have a penis and testes, they stay about the same size from the time you are a toddler until the time puberty officially begins. But once your brain signals each testicle to start making testosterone, you'll move right into stage 2, the one when things begin to change.

Stage 2: It's Official

Stage 2 is the real starting line for puberty. For most boys and kids like Kimi, it typically begins sometime between the ages of 9 and 14, but the average age is around 10. This important occasion seems like it would be obvious, but truthfully, it's usually hidden because the changes start between the legs.

First, the testes begin to grow larger as they start making testosterone. As each testicle grows, the scrotum stretches and eventually looks darker in color. Around the same time, the penis begins to grow longer. And during all of this change, a few pubic hairs may show up at the base of the penis.

Later in stage 2, erections start happening more often because of the increasing amount of testosterone.

Wait, what?

Erection Section

Let's talk about erections for a minute, just so you have the facts.

The word *erect* means "tall and straight," and that's exactly what the penis looks like with an erection. An **erection** happens when the penis becomes firm or hard and sticks up. But puberty isn't the first time erections happen. Babies and younger kids have them too! For babies, erections are common when they have to pee or when they play with their penis. Erections can happen sometimes during childhood, but during puberty, they happen a lot more because of testosterone.

> **FUN FACT:**
> Human testicles are smaller than chimpanzee testicles but larger than gorilla testicles. That tells you that bigger animals don't always have bigger "balls."

Do you wonder how an erection happens? Inside the penis, the urethra passes through the middle. On each side of the urethra, there are tubelike areas that are filled with spongy stuff. Each of those tubes has blood vessels next to it. An erection happens when those blood vessels release blood into the spongy area. This blood fills the penis so tight that the penis becomes hard and erect. But don't worry, the blood doesn't come out of the penis. It just fills up the spongy space, then it goes back into the blood vessels where it came from. Once it goes back, the erection goes away.

During puberty, erections can happen at totally random times and for no obvious reason; that's called having a **spontaneous erection.** It's sort of like blushing. Sometimes you know what will make you blush, and sometimes you have no idea. Erections can be like that!

A lot of people think erections happen only if someone is thinking about something sexy, but there are lots of other things that might trigger one. If you have a penis, you might get an erection because you see something that excites you, like a fast shiny new car. You might get an erection if you are sitting on something that is vibrating or tickling your genitals, like a running car or even the school bus. And it's true that if you discover you have special feelings for someone, you can get an erection just by thinking about them or being around them. It's totally normal to have spontaneous erections. Another thing that's common is waking up with an erection, even every day. So hopefully, it's clear: During puberty, erections are really, really common. You don't have a lot of control over when they do or don't happen.

When you have a surprise erection (and you will), it might feel embarrassing. First, you need to know that other people probably can't see it and probably have no idea it's happening. Second, you need to know that it won't last long! But if you're worried that others can see it, there are some things you can do to make it less obvious.

- If you are sitting, don't stand.
- If you have to stand, untuck your shirt or carry a book or backpack in front of you.
- Put your hand into your pocket to hold your penis down or to keep it pushed up against your body.
- If you are in a swimsuit, stay in the water or grab a towel.
- Go to a private place, like a restroom.

You may also find that erections do not show as much if you're wearing briefs instead of boxers. You'll notice that an erection goes away faster if you take your mind off it or think about something unrelated, like multiplication tables. It's normal to be bothered by erections. It's also normal to enjoy them. Sometimes that feeling just depends on the situation you're in when they happen.

As you grow older and progress through puberty, you won't have as many random erections. But in the early and middle stages of puberty, it's good to know what to expect and how to manage them.

FUN FACT:
Some people call an erection a "boner," but there's actually no bone in the penis!

Stage 3: Growing

As someone moves into stage 3, things start to look a lot different. Yes, there's more growth around the genitals, but it's also the time when arms and legs are growing fastest, and even the voice box is growing!

GROWTH CHART

4 MONTHS!

4 YEARS

In stage 3, the penis grows longer, the glans (head) of the penis may look darker in color, and pubic hair fills in. Along with those changes, the testes continue to grow and the scrotum becomes more wrinkly and darker in color. You may also notice that one testicle hangs lower than the other. That's a nice way to keep them from bumping together. You might be interested to know that it is more common for the left testicle to hang lower than the right one. But, just like being right or left handed, it's totally normal for either testicle to hang lower.

The scrotum also takes on another job as a temperature regulator to keep the testes happy and healthy. Testes need to stay at a special temperature to work their best, and that temperature is a little cooler than the normal body temperature. That means when the normal temperature is hot, the scrotum will hang a little lower to allow the testes to cool off. If it's cold, the scrotum pulls in closer to the body to warm them up. This response may seem really interesting or kind of strange, but it's actually important for you to learn about so you can understand how the body works.

Voice Changes

Along with genital changes during this time, testosterone causes more facial hair (we talked about that in Chapter 4); may cause more acne and blackheads; and causes some changes you can hear. Have you ever noticed how someone's voice may start to crack or deepen in puberty?

As the body grows, testosterone makes the voice box grow bigger and faster too. The voice box, also called the **larynx** (LAIR inks), is the bony bump in the middle of the neck. Some people call it the "Adam's apple." As the larynx grows, the vocal cords stretch. At first, the stretching makes them thinner, and that thinning causes the voice to make funny sounds people call "cracks," "breaks," or "squeaks." Sometimes people laugh at others' voice cracks, but these cracks are no reason for teasing. Remember, EVERY body has new things happening in puberty, so it's important to be kind and treat others the way you want to be treated.

The good news is that these voice cracks last only a few months because testosterone also makes the vocal cords grow thicker. That's how testosterone makes the voice deeper. Think of vocal cords like guitar strings. The thinner ones make a higher sound, and the thicker ones make a lower, deeper sound.

Stage 4: Making Sperm

During stage 4, the penis may continue to grow a little longer, but it's also growing wider now. The head of the penis also becomes a little larger. The testes may hang even lower, and the scrotum may look darker in color. As all of these changes are happening, the body begins to make sperm.

Remember that everyone goes through puberty so they can develop adult bodies that are able to reproduce and continue the human species. Making a new human is a pretty big deal. To make a new human, it takes a special cell from a male and a special cell from a female. *Sperm* is the name of the cell that comes from the male body.

Once the testes start making sperm, they continue to make a LOT of sperm—MILLIONS of sperm—every single day for many, many years into old age. That sounds like a lot of work!

Sperm are tiny cells that look like tadpoles—really, really tiny tadpoles. They have a rounded head, and they have a longer section, called a *tail,* that allows them to swim. They are so small that you could not see them without a microscope.

FUN FACT:
About 100 MILLION sperm can fit into a teaspoon.

The Journey of the Sperm

Once sperm are made in the testes, they move into the epididymis, where they spend a little time maturing and learning how to swim (kind of like their own growing-up time). Eventually, the epididymis becomes too crowded, and the mature sperm have to go somewhere to make room for the new sperm.

Sometimes, the older sperm shrivel up and dissolve, but other times, they travel out of the body through the penis. It's a long journey from the testes to the outside world. Let's recap the journey of the sperm that we mentioned in Chapter 3.

Sperm are made in the testes and stored in the epididymis. When it's time to leave the body,

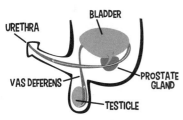

sperm travel through the vas deferens and gather fluids from the prostate gland and **seminal vesicles.** The fluids make it easier for the sperm to swim (You can't swim without water, can you?), and they also provide nutrients for the journey (like the snacks and hydration you need for a lot of exercise). The sperm and the fluids together are called *semen*. When semen squirts out of the urethra during an erection, it's called **ejaculation** (ee jack u LAY shun).

> **FUN FACT:**
> Sperm cells swim about 0.2 meters per hour, or about 8 inches. That's a lot faster than it sounds, considering how tiny they are!

But here's something important to know: ejaculation can happen only when the penis is erect, but an erection doesn't always lead to an ejaculation. In fact, there are many more erections than ejaculations.

Wait, so when *does* ejaculation happen?

If you have a penis, there are several ways ejaculation can happen. Sometimes it happens when you are touching or playing with your penis in a way that causes an erection and eventually leads to ejaculation (this is called **masturbation** [mas ter BAY shun], and there's more about it in Chapter 11). Other times, it can happen while you are sleeping. That's called a **nocturnal emission** or a **wet dream.** A wet dream is totally normal, but it can surprise you the first time it happens. If you are in one of the later stages of puberty and you wake up with a wet spot in your underwear

or on your bedsheets, you can bet you had a wet dream. How do you know you didn't pee in your bed? It will smell different than pee does, and it's only a few teaspoons of fluid—a lot less than when you pee. If you have a wet dream, it's good to take the sheets off your bed and wash them. If you don't change your sheets, dried semen can make them feel stiff and have an odor. Sometimes growing up means learning new tasks, like doing your own laundry!

Obviously, urine (pee) and semen share the same exit from the penis but never at the same time. In fact, there's a special valve that allows only one fluid to go through the urethra at a time. So how cool is that? Your body is made in such an amazing way. You can't pee and ejaculate at the same time, just like you can't breathe and swallow at the same time (You're trying to breathe and swallow right now, aren't you?).

Stage 5: The Penis Is Fully Grown

The end of puberty is stage 5, which happens when the body and all its parts are adult sized, including the penis and scrotum. How big exactly is an adult-sized penis? Lots of people wonder whether their penis is a normal size. It's important to know that penises come in all different shapes and sizes, but they all work the same (This wondering is like the way some people worry about the size of their breasts, but the size doesn't affect the way they work!). And despite

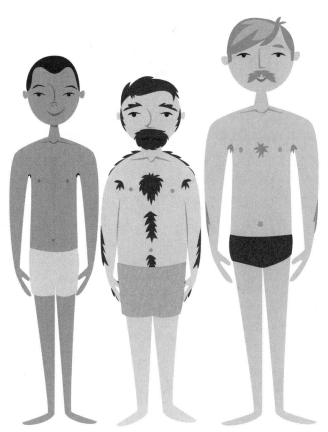

what some kids may say, the size of a penis is not at all related to the size of a person's other body parts. Maybe some of you have heard that penis size is related to hand size, foot size, or even ear size! None of that thinking is true. Also, the size of the penis has nothing to do with how masculine someone is.

The average full-grown penis (when it is NOT erect) is 3½ to 4 inches. With an erection, the average length is 5 to 5½ inches. There's no need to pull out a ruler because being larger or smaller than average doesn't matter. There is no size or shape that makes one penis better or worse than another.

Just remember, we all come in different shapes and sizes (including penises), and that's a good thing!

Did you know we need special gear for some of our body changes? Oliver goes shopping for some in the next chapter!

CHAPTER 10

PUBERTY GEAR

OLIVER

t's Friday, and the store is bustling with people. Nancy, Jazmin, and I wander the aisles, buying items for our bonfire tonight at Jazmin's house.

My hands are full of chocolate and marshmallows, while Nancy carries the graham crackers and Jazmin holds a plastic container of fruit salad. David, my older brother, even promised to teach us a few campfire songs that he learned last summer.

We wander the aisles while we wait for Jazmin's dads to grab some cleaning supplies they need. When we pass by the bra section, Nancy ushers Jazmin and me into one of the aisles.

"I can't wait to be able to wear a bra like this," Nancy says, pointing to a bright pink bra with small cups and lacey straps. She sighs. "I want to have one in every color and pattern in the world."

"That's a lot of colors and patterns," I say, laughing.

"I've started to wear them," Jazmin says. She points over to a rack of bras with stretchy fabric and thicker straps. "But I like wearing sports bras, whether I'm playing sports or not."

"Oh, fun!" Nancy says. "Those come in lots of colors and patterns too."

Jazmin nods. "I have a purple one with stars on it. But I also like my black and white ones because they blend well under my clothes."

"I have a sports bra too," I say. "I just wear the small ones. Or a binder."

"What's a binder?" Jazmin asks.

"It's a tight wrap that makes my chest look flat under my shirts. Binders come in different colors too."

"But what about patterns?" Nancy asks.

I laugh. "I'm sure there are some with patterns, but I prefer solid colors."

Nancy stares longingly at the bras. "My mom never wears bras. But she said I can when I start to feel like I need them. I can't wait for that to happen."

I point at the wide variety of bras around us. "Well, just look at all the choices you'll have when it does!"

Nancy nods and then gets distracted by something down the aisle. "Look! More cute patterns!" She skips toward a rack of pajamas. Jazmin and I share a smile before following close behind.

By now, you know that puberty may require some special items to keep your body feeling good and staying healthy! We've already discussed using deodorant, soap, razors, and maybe acne creams. And some kids will need to use period products. All these items are all called *personal care products,* and they can be important. But there are also some things you may need that we call "gear." Just like you may need special equipment or gear to stay safe, feel comfortable, and perform well in sports, you can use puberty gear to help you stay safe and comfortable through puberty.

Some body parts have built-in protection. Your rib cage protects your heart and lungs, your skull protects your brain, and your muscles protect your stomach. But what about breasts or a penis and testes?

Puberty gear is mostly about taking care of those parts, especially after they start growing. If you think about it, breasts, penises, and testes are a little freer and a little less protected than most other body parts. That's why there's gear like bras and athletic cups for your growing and sometimes sensitive parts.

WATCH THE CROTCH

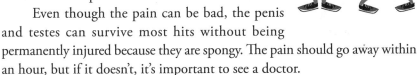

Let's start with penises and testes. Because of their loose location hanging on the outside of the body, they can get hit, bumped, or kicked pretty easily. If you have those parts and have ever been hit there, you know how much it can hurt. If you don't have testes or you've never been hit there, most people describe being hit there as a horrible pain, like being kicked in the stomach by a horse. Ouch! Sometimes the pain can be so bad it makes a person feel like they need to throw up.

Even though the pain can be bad, the penis and testes can survive most hits without being permanently injured because they are spongy. The pain should go away within an hour, but if it doesn't, it's important to see a doctor.

If you are ever hit hard in the testes or penis, try these things to make it feel better.

- Stop playing.
- Lie down.
- Bend your knees, or pull them up toward your belly.
- Place an ice pack over your testes.
- If it's OK with your parent or guardian, you may want to take a pain reliever such as ibuprofen.

You should call your doctor if any of the following things happen:

- The pain worsens or lasts more than an hour.
- You notice bruising or swelling.
- You have a difficult time going to the bathroom (to urinate, or pee).
- Your urine (pee) looks pink or bloody.

Straps and Compression

If you have a penis and you are involved in team sports, your coach may tell you to wear compression shorts so you're more comfortable. It's definitely challenging to run fast if your penis and scrotum are swinging or slapping around uncomfortably. Compression shorts keep that from happening.

You may already know about compression shorts. They are soft shorts that are tight but stretchy, and they hold the penis and scrotum snug to the body. A jockstrap is another type of compression that has an elastic waistband with a mesh pocket for the penis and scrotum and elastic straps for holding everything in close. Most people find compression shorts more comfortable, and they're definitely more popular today. Compression shorts are also sometimes worn by some transgender girls and nonbinary kids who want to make their genitals look smoother or less noticeable.

Whichever you choose, it's important to make sure you have the right size. If your compression isn't snug, your gear is not doing its job.

FUN FACT:
Folks decided a long time ago that it was important to protect their genitals. The first jockstrap was invented in 1874 to provide comfort and support for men riding bicycles on the cobblestone streets of Boston.

The Importance of Cups

In some sports, it's also important to use an **athletic cup** for pure protection. An athletic cup is a smooth curved piece of hard plastic that protects the penis and testes from injury. There's no need to use an athletic cup for just hanging around or running, but it's important in contact sports that involve a ball, a puck, or another flying object. In these types of activities, an athletic cup is as important as a helmet and mouth guard. In fact, the following sports leagues usually require athletic cups for anyone with a penis:

FUN FACT:
The athletic cup protects your testes, but it's not indestructible. Legendary Cincinnati Reds catcher, Johnny Bench, proved that. During his career, baseballs broke 7 of his cups. Talk about "breaking balls"!

- Football
- Baseball
- Hockey
- Lacrosse

Putting a Cup On

If you need to wear an athletic cup, you'll also need to wear compression shorts. You can't wear just the cup inside of boxers or briefs. You don't want the cup directly against your skin because it will rub and cause irritation. Compression shorts have a pocket or pouch the cup can slide into. Aha! That's what the pocket is for!

Wearing an athletic cup may feel strange at first because you have to make sure your penis and testes are placed correctly. Point the skinny end of the cup downward between your legs, then insert it into the pouch of the compression shorts. As you pull on the shorts, lift your penis and testes up, then place them comfortably inside the cup as you press the cup against your body. Your compression shorts will hold the cup in the correct position.

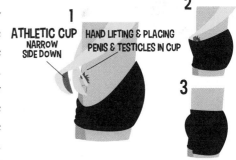

Once you get used to putting on your cup, it should become as routine as putting on your helmet or other safety gear. Just pay attention to how your penis is growing because you'll need bigger-sized cups throughout puberty. If your cup is too small, it can pinch and it won't protect you!

ARE YOU A "BOOBIE" NEWBIE?

As breasts grow in puberty, they also become body parts that are a bit more free and loose. As that change happens, it usually makes people think about wearing a bra. Although wearing a bra is a personal choice, most people feel more comfortable, supported, and more covered in one.

Some kids are embarrassed about wearing a bra because they don't want anyone to know that they're developing breasts. Some kids are excited to wear a bra. Remember that EVERY body changes during puberty, so you, your friends, and all the other kids around your age are in this together. If you are developing breasts, wearing a bra may feel new or uncomfortable at first, but before long, you'll get used to it!

When is it time to wear a bra? If you're not sure whether it's time to wear a bra, you might want to ask for advice from someone else you know and trust who wears one. Here are some answers we received from other kids about when *they* decided it was time.

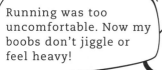

Running was too uncomfortable. Now my boobs don't jiggle or feel heavy!

I asked my mom for a bra when my friends started wearing them.

I went bra shopping when I realized my breasts showed through my clothes.

Bra Shopping

How do you feel about going shopping for a bra? Embarrassed? Excited? Just another chore? Everyone has different feelings about it. If you don't want to look at bras in a store, maybe your parent or another adult you trust can bring some home for you to try on in the privacy of your own room. If they do, make sure to leave the tags on and save the receipt so they can return the ones you don't like. If you are excited, make bra shopping a fun trip with your parent or another adult who likes to take you shopping.

FUN FACT:
The first bra was invented in 1914 by Mary Phelps Jacobs, who called it a *brassiere* (bra ZEER).

Breast Gear

Some kids like to start their bra wearing with a tank top or *cami* (short for *camisole*) that has a built-in bra. Others prefer the security of a sports bra that prevents their breasts from jiggling or makes their breasts look smaller. Some like to wear a bra with a little padding that keeps their nipples from showing. Some like lacey bras, and some think lacey bras are too itchy. Some never want to wear a bra. But for many people, there comes a time when wearing a bra is more comfortable than not wearing one.

If you think you're ready for a bra, it's easy to start off with a stretchy cami or sports bra. These are comfortable and fit even the smallest breasts. Once your breasts grow more (stages 3, 4, and 5; see Chapter 7), it will be important to buy the correct size so your gear is doing its job of keeping you comfortable.

Size Matters

Although breast size doesn't matter, bra sizes do because there are lots of different sizes, and finding the right size can be confusing. Some bras come in small, medium, large, and extra-large sizes. Others are sized like clothes: 8, 10, 12, 14, 16, and so on. And others have sizes that use letters and a number, like 34B, 32A, or 40DD. Huh?

It's easiest to start with the simple sizes that match your clothing size. You want to make sure your entire breast is inside the stretchy part or the rounded parts, called *cups*. If your breasts stick out below the bra band or overflow the top of

the bra, you need a larger cup size. A bra that is too small will be uncomfortable and will not provide good support for your growing breasts. A bra that fits and supports breasts well not only is more comfortable but also may reduce the stretch marks that grow on breasts (we focus more on stretch marks in Chapter 13).

FUN FACT: The average American woman owns 6 bras, with one of those being a strapless bra.

The sizes with letters and numbers work for some smaller breasts, but they are mostly for larger breast sizes later in puberty and into adulthood. If you need a larger bra and the sizes are confusing, you can always get measured at a bra store. The people working there have been trained to measure and fit bras correctly. They can help you find one that fits just right.

Bra Vocabulary

It's no surprise that there are lots and lots of different types of bras out there. Check out the following box to learn about some of them:

shelf bra—This natural bra is built into a *cami* (short for *camisole*) or other clothing. It looks like a cami on the outside, but there's a bra on the inside.

training bra—This bra doesn't really "train" anything; it just helps someone get used to wearing a bra. A training bra is a small bra, usually with a cup size of A, AA, or AAA (small, smaller, or smallest).

binder—A binder is an undershirt in the style of a tank top or tube top (a top with no straps) that is made of very tight and stretchy fabric. A binder helps the chest look flatter, so it can be helpful for kids like Oliver.

sports bra—This type of bra usually pulls over the head and fits pretty snug. It keeps breasts from bouncing around and hurting during active times or sports. Some people like to wear these bras all the time, not just for sports.

strapless bra—This bra has no straps! Exactly like its name says! People choose this whenever they're wearing strapless, halter, or thin-strapped tops or anytime they don't want bra straps to show. Without straps, though, this can slide off the breasts during running or very active times, so it's not recommended in those situations.

padded bra—This bra has some padding built into the cups. Some kids wear these bras because the pads keep their nipples from showing through their shirt, make their clothes fit better, or make their breasts look a little larger.

underwire bra—This bra has a piece of hard plastic or wire under the cup. The wire helps support the breasts and keeps them from slipping below the cup. Underwires are used mostly for larger breast sizes.

push-up bra—This bra pushes breasts up and in to make them look fuller in the middle and create **cleavage,** which is the line that forms between the breasts if they are large enough to meet in the middle. Breasts don't squish together in the middle naturally. It takes padding, wires, and pushing to create cleavage.

ze-bra—A black-and-white–striped bra. Just kidding!

Obviously, there are different styles of bras that people may choose for different styles of tops. Below, **match** the top with the bra that might work best.

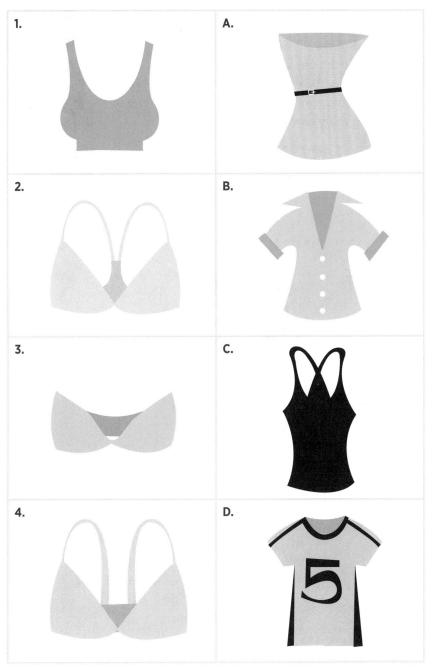

GEAR FOR ALL!

So now you know that EVERY body is changing and EVERY body can use gear, like equipment and clothing, to keep their growing body safe and comfortable in all sorts of situations. If you need an athletic cup, compression shorts, or a bra, hopefully you feel better knowing the options and how to use them. Always remember that the adults who care for you can help you with your puberty gear needs!

I've learned so much, but I still have some questions. Should I search the internet? Jack has some thoughts on that in the next chapter.

CHAPTER 11

CURIOSITY

JACK

Leshaun, Antonio, Stephanie, and I are at Leshaun's house, working together on our group science project. Antonio is sitting in front of the computer, and the rest of us are circled around him with our notebooks in our laps. We're supposed to be answering questions about animals' bodies, but Antonio suddenly lands on a website that seems wrong for our research.

"Whoa," Antonio says, "I think this article is actually about the human body."

"That's not an article," Stephanie says, squinting at the screen. "What do those words even mean?"

"Try that link at the bottom," Leshaun says. "That looks like it could answer question number 5."

"Hey, wait a second," I say, putting down my notebook, "that doesn't look scientific to me. I think we should get off this website."

"This is scientific!" Antonio says, starting to scroll down toward some photographs.

"Gross, are those naked people? What are they doing?" Leshaun says.

"I really don't want to see any more of that stuff," I say. "And I don't think any of you do either. Let's just go back to the Science Kids site and stick to that. There are some really weird things on the internet that we probably want to stay away from."

"Jack's right," Stephanie says. "I've made a mistake with that before and seen something I wish I hadn't. It's not worth it."

"OK," Antonio says, clicking the back button away from the website. "But how will we do assignments like this one when we learn about the human body? If there's so much bad stuff on the internet, how will we know what the facts are?"

"I know there's a section on the human body in our textbooks," Leshaun says. "I was looking ahead to see what else we're going to learn this year and I saw it."

"And Mr Okoro loves to help people pick out books in the library," Stephanie says. "When I wanted to learn about muscles for dance, he sent me home with a stack so big that I could barely carry it."

Antonio nods. I point to a link on the Science Kids website.

"Here's a timeline on how tadpoles grow into frogs," I say. "Isn't that what question number 7 is about?"

"Good one, Jack," Antonio says, clicking on it. And we fill out our assignment, back on track.

One thing we know about kids your age is that you are a pretty curious bunch. As you enter puberty and see your friends' bodies changing, it's normal to be curious. You may wonder whether your body is changing in the same ways as your friends'. You may wonder about other kids' changing bodies or even about adult bodies. And now that you know about the private parts on EVERY body, you may also be curious to explore more about yourself.

CURIOUS ABOUT YOURSELF

Exploring your body and how it works helps you understand it and take care of it. So if you're curious about your private parts, that's perfectly normal and OK. Your body is yours, and you should definitely be familiar with all its parts!

We mentioned back in Chapter 3 that it's a good idea to grab a mirror, find a private place, and take a look at your genitals so you know what they look like. But what if you want to touch them? That's OK too! You'll probably

find that it feels good to touch them. In fact, even as a baby, you probably discovered that touching yourself there felt nice.

When you touch your private parts in a way that feels good, that's called *masturbation*. You may know that word, and you may have heard other silly phrases for it. Maybe people use those phrases because they feel awkward when using the real word. Sometimes kids even joke or tease each other about masturbating. There are also some myths out there that you'll go blind or grow hair on your hands if you masturbate. Those are definitely false!

The truth is that masturbation feels good and it's normal. EVERY body has special nerves around their genitals that make certain areas extra sensitive to touch. But even though masturbation is normal, we have a few recommendations for you.

- It's not something to chat about with people you don't know well because most people consider it private and personal.
- It's definitely a private activity and should happen only when you're alone in a private place like your bedroom or bathroom.
- It should not take up most of your free time.

If you follow those simple rules, masturbation is a normal and healthy way to get to know your body, whether you have a penis or a vulva.

If you have a penis, touching or rubbing yourself in a way that feels good often leads to an erection and possibly to ejaculation. The intense good feeling that happens with ejaculation is called an **orgasm** (OR gaz um). Masturbation can feel good with or without an orgasm.

If you have a vulva, masturbation is similar, except for the ejaculation part. Touching your clitoris or genitals can also feel good and can lead to an orgasm as well. Although there's no ejaculation, the vagina may put out a little fluid that is more than its normal discharge, but nothing squirts out.

So when it comes to your own body, curiosity is normal and healthy. Masturbation is also totally up to you. It's normal if you masturbate, it's normal if you don't.

FUN FACT:

Animals masturbate too. Deer, monkeys, walruses, and squirrels have all been documented as masturbating.

CURIOUS ABOUT OTHERS

What about being curious about other people's bodies? The human body is supercool, and many people are especially curious about other people's parts that are usually covered. But because those parts are private, it can be hard to find a safe and healthy way to explore that curiosity.

Sometimes, you might see partly naked bodies of people in swimsuits when you're at the beach. You might see big posters of models in fancy bras and underwear in the windows of stores that sell those things. Some movies show naked people, but those movies are only for adults.

So what about the internet? You can find anything there, can't you? But wait! Let's talk about the internet for a minute. It's a very tricky place!

THE INTERNET

The most important thing you need to remember about the internet is that there are no rules about what can be put there. Anybody can post anything. That means there is no person or group checking to see whether everything on the internet is true. Nobody checks to see whether things are appropriate for children. Nobody removes the stuff that is not appropriate. People can put anything on the internet, and there are no police or rules that keep it safe. That is why many parents and schools have their own rules about how, when, and where you are allowed to use the internet.

Think about this: What happens when there are no rules? What if there were no rules in soccer? Or in volleyball? Or at school? People would misbehave and get hurt. A lack of rules would create a lot of problems. Well, on the internet, there are basically no rules, so there are definitely things there that aren't meant for kids, aren't safe for kids, and could scare or even hurt kids.

In particular, there are pictures or videos called **pornography (porn)** that you may have heard of. Pornography involves photos or videos of naked people (they're usually actors) doing stuff with their naked bodies that is very different from what most people do with their naked bodies. Pornography is wrong and harmful to kids because it gives the wrong information. It often shows people being hurt, and most of it is very disrespectful to women and even men. Most of all, it can confuse you by making you think some things are OK that aren't really OK. It can also teach you stuff that is wrong and hurtful to yourself and others. And it can give you very wrong ideas of what it means to be an adult. Many of the pictures can be disturbing. Pornography can be like a scary scene in a movie. Once you see it, it's hard to unsee and forget it.

WHAT IF I SEE IT?

But if you're like most kids who spend time on the internet, you might land on pornography at some point. Landing on it may have already happened to you. Sometimes, it just pops up on your screen when you are looking for other stuff. Other times, you may search for something that accidentally takes you there.

If so, it's always best to close the screen and let a parent or another adult you trust know what happened. Don't click on any other buttons on the screen.

What you see may shock or scare you. Most of all, know that if you are seeing pornography, it is not the way normal people act. Even the bodies don't look normal because many of the people have had surgeries to make themselves look a certain way, or the images have been changed to look different from those of most healthy bodies. The internet is no place to learn about naked or changing bodies. By turning it off, you'll keep yourself from believing false information. If you want true and accurate information about changing bodies, there are much better and safer places to find that information.

SAFE WAYS

So if you are curious (And remember, it's OK and very normal to be curious!), there are other things you can do. There are safe books you can look through. Your local library has books your parent or guardian can check out. Many books about art have naked bodies. There are also science and nature books that have illustrations or pictures of the naked human body. It might be embarrassing to ask if you can see pictures of naked people, but seeing them in a safe book is a lot better than seeing pornography.

Obviously, you want accurate and truthful information. You want to know what's real. You want to know the facts. Talking with your parents or trusted caregivers is the best way to learn, so if you want to see pictures, you need to ask them to guide you so you can get that information in a way that helps you learn and feel comfortable but doesn't harm you.

REAL–LIFE NUDITY

Every family is different when it comes to being naked in front of each other. Some parents don't close the door when they are getting dressed. Some families share a bathroom and see each other getting in and out of the shower. Other families encourage closed doors and privacy when it comes to naked times. Within your family, seeing each other's naked bodies can be normal if everyone is comfortable with that.

Outside of families, though, you shouldn't be seeing other naked bodies or showing yours. It's one thing to change clothes in a locker room with other kids or to change them in front of your best friends. Some kids feel comfortable with changing clothes in front of each other. Some don't. Either feeling is totally normal. But if you or one of your friends is going out of their way to see or show naked bodies, that can be a problem because it ignores the importance of privacy, and it can be disrespectful. If any adults are trying to see young people's naked bodies or show their own, that's an even bigger problem.

PRIVACY MATTERS

Why is the privacy thing so important? Sometimes there are people (very wrong people) who want to look at or touch kid's genitals, have kids look at or touch theirs, or even show them pictures or movies of naked bodies. Sometimes these people are other kids. Sometimes they are even family members or someone you know and trust.

What they're doing is wrong and against the law, and it's called **sexual abuse.** Because it's wrong, they often try to talk kids into keeping it a secret.

Sometimes they trick kids into thinking it's a game. They might even scare kids into blaming themselves for doing something bad or into fearing that they will get into trouble.

Again, sexual abuse is very, very wrong and against the law. If anyone ever tries to involve you in something like this, it's really important to tell an adult you trust. If it has happened to you, it's not your fault, and you won't get into trouble for it. Telling an adult can make it stop and keep the person from doing that to you and any other kids too. Don't ever keep it a secret.

TOO CURIOUS?

What if you feel like you need to put pressure on other kids or talk them into letting you see or touch their private parts? That's a problem too. Putting pressure on others is different from just being curious.

If you become so curious that you frequently try to see or touch naked bodies of friends or other kids, or if you know of a friend who's doing that, it's super important to tell an adult or your doctor. That way, you can learn how this behavior may harm you and the other kids involved and you can find safer ways to manage your curiosity.

TALKING WITH ADULTS

Most of the time, curiosity is a wonderful thing. It's a great way to learn and often leads to big discoveries. Sometimes, though, both kids and adults can cross the line from showing healthy curiosity to breaking boundaries that lead to disrespectful or even harmful behaviors. In this chapter, we've discussed some healthy ways to explore your curiosity about bodies and some problems that can happen when people go beyond curiosity.

A lot of parents and other caring adults don't talk with children about the topics of pornography or sexual abuse. Sometimes they don't talk about these things because they think the topic might scare you or they don't know how to start the conversation. But even if they don't bring it up, it's really important for you to tell them whether you or a friend have ever experienced sexual abuse or felt uncomfortable about anything to do with your body. If you don't feel comfortable with telling a parent, then another trusted adult, like a teacher or counselor, can help.

Many adults don't bring up the topic of masturbation with kids either. They may want to respect your privacy or are not sure how to talk about it with you. Maybe you and the important adults in your life will break that trend and have a healthy conversation about masturbation. If you want to talk more about any of these topics but don't know how to start, just hand them this book and point to this chapter.

I'm pretty excited for puberty, but Kimi isn't. Keep reading to find out why.

CHAPTER 12

WHEN PUBERTY DOESN'T FEEL RIGHT

KIMI

Quinn, Jazmin, Nancy, and I are getting ready for bed, stepping around the sleeping bags that form a circle on Nancy's bedroom floor. I take my pajamas to the corner and turn my back to the others as I change. Quinn is changing at the same time and isn't paying attention, and Jazmin is looking for something in her bag, but then Nancy looks over at me right as I'm changing my shirt.

I try to cover my chest, and Nancy looks away quickly, but I know she saw my flat chest. She must see how uncomfortable I am because she speaks up quickly.

"I still have a super flat chest too," Nancy says. She keeps her eyes on her own clothes, but I know she's talking to me. "I can't wait to finally start puberty. I hate blooming so much later than everyone else."

I finish putting on my pajamas and then take a deep breath. "My body will never grow breasts on its own because I'm trans," I say, looking at Nancy until she meets my eyes. "But it's something that I have options for and that I talk with my doctor about."

"I didn't know," Nancy says, and Quinn and Jazmin both nod in agreement.

"Thanks for telling us. We won't tell anyone else," Quinn says. Then Quinn explains that they don't identify as a boy or a girl, so they know what it's like to get questions about gender expectations. "I talk with my doctor about being nonbinary, too. It's nice to have someone who can help my parents and me figure out what is going to work best for my body."

I nod, feeling a rush of relief at someone who understands.

We all finish changing and settle down on our sleeping bags, facing each other in the middle of the circle.

"I am still a late bloomer with the puberty stuff, Nancy," I say, smiling. "So I know how you feel."

"I felt like I was the first one to start puberty," Jazmin says. "And my little sister Jada just started talking with me about her puberty changes, even though she's 2 years younger than we are."

"Wow," Quinn says, "I kind of thought everyone went through it at the same time."

"Everyone's different," I say. I narrow my eyes at Quinn. "Just like you like pineapple on your pizza even though it's the grossest thing in the world."

"Hey!" Quinn exclaims. "It's the best topping!"

Nancy shakes her head. "I'm with you, Kimi. I think it's gross."

"You're both just late bloomers on realizing how great puberty is," Jazmin says. "One day, you'll come around." She grins and looks around at the group. "And pineapple is the best pizza topping!"

Are you the type of person who loves experiencing new things? Or do you feel more comfortable when things stay the same and feel familiar? Sometimes it's exciting and fun to have new experiences, but big changes can make some people feel annoyed, uneasy, confused, or even panicked. By now, you know that the years during puberty will be full of big changes in your body and your mind. Some kids are happy with their growing and changing body. Some kids hardly notice the changes or don't seem to care. And for some kids, the changes happening (or not happening) during puberty just don't feel right at all. There are several different reasons why this feeling may happen.

TOO EARLY

Being the first one to try something new can be stressful, especially when you didn't ask for the experience. If you are the very first kid in your grade to have puberty changes, it can feel too early, even though these changes may be normal. We mentioned already that it can be normal for breasts to bud as young as the age of 8 or for testes to start growing as young as the age of 9, but for some children, signs of puberty can show up even earlier.

Some kids with early puberty have only breast growth. Some have only body odor and pubic hair growth, without other changes of puberty. And sometimes, all the puberty changes start happening to a child who is just way too young.

When signs of puberty happen earlier than the typical age, doctors call it **precocious** (pre CO shus) **puberty.** *Precocious* means showing development or maturity that is farther along than expected for someone's age. Most of the time, precocious puberty is not a serious medical problem, but occasionally, it can be caused by health problems that need treatment. That's why kids with early puberty should see their doctor, who will test for health problems and help their families decide whether it's a good idea to stop puberty for a while.

FUN FACT:

Precocious puberty is 10 times more common in kids with ovaries than in kids with testes. But for all kids, puberty is starting younger than it did 100 years ago.

Wait, what? Doctors can put puberty on pause? That's true. Doctors can prescribe medicine to stop puberty temporarily. But they do that *only* for important reasons. Early puberty can cause emotional and physical problems for very young children. It can be difficult for very young kids to manage puberty, and early puberty can stunt their growth. For those reasons, doctors may use certain medications to pause puberty. Then, when the child is older, they can stop the medicine, and puberty will begin again. At that point, puberty will progress normally, like it does for others. Some people refer to those medications as *puberty blockers,* but really, they don't block puberty forever; they just put puberty on pause.

LATE BLOOMERS

You know what else can feel stressful? When you expect something to happen but it doesn't. If all your friends are experiencing changes of puberty and you are still rocking a child's body, it can feel like something's wrong even though it may be considered totally normal. On the other hand, you might be relieved that you don't have to deal with all the puberty stuff yet.

Remember, breasts should bud before the age of 13 (see Chapter 7), periods should start before turning 16 (see Chapter 8), and testes typically begin to grow before the age of 15 (see Chapter 9). If those events haven't started by those ages, your doctor would want to know. And sometimes, puberty may start at a normal time but then stall. For example, after breasts bud, menstruation, which should start within 3 years, may not. If puberty is blooming later or more slowly than it does for most kids, your doctor can help you and your family figure out why.

Most commonly, puberty is late because that delay runs in the family. If your biological parents or siblings were late bloomers, you may be too.

If it's not related to your genetics, sometimes the delay is simply because your brain and body are still figuring out how to use your hormones to communicate better with your ovaries or testes. That process can take time.

Sometimes, though, puberty can start late or stop progressing because of illnesses. If you have a chronic health condition, like diabetes, cancer, an autoimmune disease, or another complicated medical condition, puberty may be delayed. When your body uses a lot of energy trying to stay healthy, it doesn't always have the extra energy to put into puberty. Often, once your medical condition is under good control, puberty will show up!

For most kids, being very thin or athletic can be another reason for delayed puberty. That's because for normal growth—especially for the menstrual cycle—to happen, the body needs to be taking in enough energy through food and storing some of that energy in fat cells. If someone is eating less food than their body needs, exercising too much, or both, their body won't grow like it's supposed to. That can slow down or delay puberty. Normal growth will start again when there's more food, less activity, or some combination of both to create better balance.

JUST NOT FEELING RIGHT

Sometimes puberty can start right on time, but the changes happening on the outside of the body don't truly feel right. Sure, lots of kids might feel a little weird or uncomfortable about their changing body, but for some kids, it's not just strange or new. For some, the changes on the outside of their body don't fit with the way they feel on the inside. Or for some, the outside changes feel completely wrong.

Remember in Chapter 3 when we defined the difference between being cisgender and transgender? If you are a cisgender boy, like Jack or Leshaun (born with a penis, feel like a boy), and suddenly, you start growing large breasts and you get a period, that would probably feel really wrong. Similarly, if you are like Stephanie or Maria, a cisgender girl, and you start growing a mustache, getting a deep voice, and growing a penis, that would feel really wrong and might even make you feel panicked. In either case, you and your parents would definitely receive help from your doctor.

FUN FACT:
Transgender people have always existed. There are some records that go back 4,500 years that show that transgender people were a part of communities way back then!

For gender-diverse kids, such as transgender or nonbinary kids, like Oliver, Kimi, or Quinn, the changes happening to their body can feel just plain wrong and can create these same big feelings. When their body changes don't match the gender they are on the inside, they may feel like their body is developing the wrong parts or their genitals don't match how they feel.

If someone experiences a lot of distress and worry because their body isn't matching their gender identity, it's called **gender dysphoria** (dis FOR ee ah). For them, talking with a doctor is important too. But not all nonbinary or transgender kids experience gender dysphoria. Some gender-diverse kids feel just fine about their body and how it's changing. They may not feel upset or distressed about the changes at all. What's most important is that everyone is supported in finding a way to feel good about their body and that everyone can express themself in a way that feels best for them.

Just like kids with early or precocious puberty, some transgender and nonbinary kids might be prescribed a medication to pause puberty. That lets them pause the changes until they work with their doctors, counselor, and family to figure out what is best for them. Once they are a little older, they may choose to stop the blocker medicine, and puberty will continue. Other gender-diverse kids may choose to begin another medication that can help their body continue with puberty in the way that feels best for them. For someone experiencing gender dysphoria, it's super-duper important to get help from a trusted and supportive team of doctors, counselors, and maybe even other people who have been through the same thing.

Whether or not they're taking medications to pause puberty, some gender-diverse kids feel better when keeping their body changes less noticeable. They may also wear clothing, hairstyles, accessories, or other gear to make their appearance match their gender identity better. Some gender-diverse kids who are developing breasts may wear sports bras or binders (called **binding**) to compress their breasts so they aren't so noticeable. Some gender-diverse kids may not want others to see the front bump that their growing penis and scrotum make. To make it less obvious, they may wear compression shorts or tuck their penis and scrotum back between their legs, which some kids call **tucking.** Although binding and tucking may make body parts less noticeable, they can be uncomfortable or harmful if done without care, so talking about them with a doctor who understands is important.

EMBRACING BIG FEELINGS

If you are having experiences in puberty that don't really feel right, we want to make sure you talk with a parent or another trusted adult because there are lots of ways they can help. Whether your puberty is early, is late, or just feels wrong, your doctor can guide you and your family. Doctors, nurses, and counselors in health care are eager to help you cope with big feelings and help you find a way to make puberty feel better and right for you.

There's a lot going on with puberty, isn't there? If we want to stay healthy, we need to know how to take care of our growing bodies! Oliver learns this lesson in the next chapter.

CHAPTER 13

STRONG AND HEALTHY BODIES

OLIVER

Nice shot!" I tell Nancy as the ball swishes through the net.

David, my older brother, leans forward to rest his hands on his knees, panting for breath. "You two have gotten faster," he says. "I can't defend you both at the same time anymore!"

Sun streams around us and reflects off the pavement court in the center of our neighborhood park. All around us, there are little kids playing on the playground, soccer games happening on the fields, and people walking and biking down the trails.

David retrieves the ball and starts dribbling toward the basket. I shuffle with him, playing defense and blocking his way to the hoop with my body. When he takes the layup and misses, I jump up into the air to grab the rebound, feeling like I'm flying.

"Now that was a high jump!" Nancy says, clapping for me.

"You've gotten taller," David says, wiping sweat from his forehead, "and stronger. Shooting over your head used to be easy!"

"Not anymore," I say, grinning. "Sure, sometimes I wake up in the night with growing pains in my legs, and sometimes I trip over my own feet at school, but my growing body can do a lot of amazing things too."

"Hey, look," Nancy says, pointing toward the soccer fields. "Is that Maria?"

I follow her gaze to where one of the soccer games has just ended and see a familiar figure walking toward us across the grass. We raise our arms to wave to her, and Maria comes running in her soccer uniform, with her bag slung over one shoulder. We jog over to meet her.

"We won!" Maria calls, and we all give her high fives. "I scored 2 goals."

"Congrats!" I tell her.

Then we notice Nancy, swaying a little on her feet, with her eyes unfocused. David puts a hand on Nancy's shoulder.

"Whoa there," he says, helping steady Nancy. "Are you OK?"

Nancy nods, slinking to the ground and putting her head between her knees. "Yeah, sorry," she says, taking deep breaths, "I just got a little dizzy running over here."

Maria pulls her bag off her shoulder and sets it onto the grass beside her. She pulls out an unopened bottle of water and a plastic bag full of orange wedges and hands them to Nancy.

"You definitely need to stay hydrated, being out in this sun," Maria says. Nancy takes a long drink from the water bottle and then sucks on an orange wedge.

"My coach always gives us extra water and fruit as a snack at our games. 'Winners fuel their bodies right!'" Maria adds.

We watch Nancy as she drinks more water; the focus quickly returns to her eyes.

"Are you feeling better?" I ask.

Nancy pops an orange wedge into her mouth and then smiles to show us an orange peel where her teeth should be. She gives a double thumbs-up.

"I think that's a yes!" David says, and we all laugh.

If puberty is all about "growing" into an adult body, there's a lot more to it than just hair and genitals, right? There's that part about growing taller and bigger. That's the part that really starts to amaze the adults in your life. One day, you are a little human always looking up at the adults around you, and within 6 months to a year, your pants are too short and you are looking eye to eye with full-sized grown-ups! It's yet another amazing accomplishment of puberty.

It's not like you haven't been growing and suddenly, in puberty, you do. It's just that you've never grown so fast! Remember that for EVERY body, the puberty growth spurt starts with your hands and feet, but once your arms and legs start growing longer, you're really on your way!

OUT AND ABOUT

And you aren't just growing up. There are times when you grow "out" more than you grow "up." For kids who have a lot of estrogen, their bodies can change shape and become curvier. It's pretty common for their hips, thighs, butt, and breasts to grow bigger and for their waist to become more obvious. But for some, their curves are not very noticeable, and that's normal too.

For kids with a lot of testosterone, it's typical to become more muscular, but it takes time. First, arms and legs do some "speed growing" and give the body an extra-long and lean look. This happens because bones grow faster than muscles, so the muscles have to stretch, which makes them look thinner or smaller. Some kids are frustrated by this stretching because they want to look stronger and more muscular, but patience is key. No matter how quickly you want your cool factor to shine, if you have plenty of testosterone circulating in your body, you will begin to look more muscular and less lanky as you reach the end of puberty. But being funny, brainy, or musical can win just as much attention as being muscular or athletic.

OUCH!

Does all that muscle stretching along with bone growing hurt? It can! Growing pains are real, and they are common during puberty. Normal growing pains feel like an ache inside your bones or muscles. If touching or squeezing an area feels painful, that's probably an injury instead of a growing pain. Also, if you have normal growing pains, the pain will be in a general area, not just one small spot you can point to with the tip of your finger.

If growing pains keep you awake at night or interfere with your activities, you should check with your doctor. If your doctor examines you and finds nothing wrong, they may recommend a mild medication like ibuprofen or acetaminophen. But always make sure you check with a parent or adult in charge before taking any medications. And if you notice pains that do not sound like normal growing pains, please see your doctor.

STRETCHY

Your skin obviously has to stretch as you grow. Usually, skin is pretty stretchy, but sometimes when you're growing super fast, your skin may develop **stretch marks.** These are groups of lines that show up on your skin. Depending on your skin color, they can look red, brown, purple, pink, dark brown, or like something in between. When they first happen, they can feel slightly raised and make your skin itch or burn. Over time, the color will fade and become a little lighter than your normal skin color.

FUN FACT: During the puberty growth spurt, kids grow about 3½ to 4 inches each year.

Almost EVERY body grows stretch marks during puberty, and many people get them in several places. They're most common on breasts, upper thighs, belly, and hips. There's not much you can do to prevent or get rid of stretch marks, but it may help to keep your skin moisturized by drinking plenty of water and using gentle lotions or creams. Just remember that there are no creams that will make stretch marks disappear (even though some brands claim they can). Eventually, these marks all become less noticeable.

Stretch marks are nothing to be concerned or embarrassed about. They're just a sign of fast growth. Think of them like your body's own racing stripes!

CLUMSY?

There's one especially awkward thing that can happen when you're growing super fast. You literally become awkward! And by that, we mean physically awkward—as in clumsy.

Here's why: during growth spurts, your bones grow first, and they grow faster than your muscles. As your muscles are pulled and stretched, they can't keep up with all the bone growth. You may trip or stumble over your own feet, lose your balance more easily, or just not have the same moves you've always had in sports or activities.

So be prepared to have some off times during your growth. These can be tough to manage, but be patient and keep practicing your moves. Once your muscles catch up with your bones (They will!) and have a chance to adjust, you'll be stronger, more coordinated, and even more skilled than you were before you grew!

HOW TALL?

Your doctor pays attention to how you're growing by checking your height regularly. Growing taller is a sign of health, but at some point, toward the very end of puberty, you will stop growing taller. Do you ever wonder how tall you'll be when you are fully grown? It's a bit of a mystery, but there are some clues!

During most of your childhood, you grew about 2 inches every year, but during puberty, you may grow 3, 4, or more inches in less than a year! For most girls and kids like Oliver, the fastest growth happens about 6 months before the first period starts, and then growth slows down pretty quickly. For most boys and kids like Kimi, it's common to grow about 3 to 4 inches every year for several years before the growing slows down.

How tall you grow depends a lot on genetics. You can look at your biological parents or siblings for an idea of how tall you might be, but there's a lot of variety in families, isn't there? If you're curious, there's no crystal ball to predict how tall you'll be, but your doctor might be able to give you a couple of clues.

One clue comes from your growth chart, which is a graph where your doctor or nurse marks your height and weight anytime you go in for a checkup. Most kids seem to stay within the same range of being average, bigger than average, or smaller than average. By using your growth chart, your doctor can show you how you've been growing, when your growth is slowing down, and how tall you are expected to be if you stay healthy.

Male Formula:
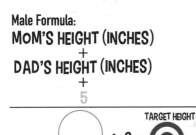
MOM'S HEIGHT (INCHES)
+
DAD'S HEIGHT (INCHES)
+
5

( ) ÷ 2 = TARGET HEIGHT

Female Formula:
MOM'S HEIGHT (INCHES)
+
DAD'S HEIGHT (INCHES)
−
5

( ) ÷ 2 = TARGET HEIGHT

The other way your doctor (and you!) can predict your height is by doing a special math problem, or formula, to predict how tall you'll be. This formula works only if you know the height of your biological parents. Although it isn't exact at all (it will predict the same exact height for you and your siblings who are the same biological sex), it's fun to try. When you calculate the answer, you'll have your predicted height in inches. It might be fun to write down your answer somewhere so you can see whether it comes true!

GROWING IS HARD WORK

So now that we've shared with you what you need to *know* about growing, let's talk about what you can *do* to help your body stay healthy and feel good while it's working hard to become your grown-up body!

Although you may not notice, your body works extra hard when you're growing. To grow well, your body needs food, water, exercise, and rest. Your body has never grown so fast (except when you were an infant). That's why puberty is an important time to develop healthy habits. Believe it or not, the healthy habits you start now will help you through the rest of your life.

Unhealthy habits (like trying to live on chocolate, ice cream, soda pop, and potato chips or never exercising) are hard to break. Healthy habits can even help you live longer. So when you help your body by giving it the stuff it needs, like delicious and nutritious foods, regular exercise, and plenty of sleep, you'll grow a look that looks and feels great on you!

FUN FACT:

A single 12-ounce can of soda pop has about 10 teaspoons of sugar. That's more than the amount of sugar that any person should have in one day if they are following recommendations for a healthy diet.

Feed Your Body

Did you notice that we recommended nutritious *and* delicious foods? Even though we're doctors and we talk a lot about healthy foods, we also believe that food should be enjoyable and fun! So if you were expecting us to tell you to eat just vegetables and not cookies or ice cream, we've got better news for you!

When it comes to health, food is the energy source for everything your body does. Just like a computer needs energy from electricity to turn on and work, EVERY body needs energy from food to do the work of living and growing. When you digest food, your body takes each bite and breaks it into smaller parts known as **nutrients.** Have you heard of proteins, carbohydrates (carbs), fats, fiber, vitamins, minerals, or antioxidants? Those are all types of nutrients, and your body needs lots of them every day. They are basically like the energy packs, building materials, and cleanup crew your body needs to grow and do all the cool things it can do. No wonder you get so hungry!

Besides providing energy, food is important for other reasons. Preparing food for others can be a way some people show they care. Sharing food with others is a great way to spend time with friends. Experimenting with new recipes is a way to be creative. Many foods help people feel connected to their culture or learn about other cultures. Some foods can even make you feel warm and fuzzy because they are just yummy or they remind you of a special person or time in your life.

Here are some food and nutrition tips that can help you feed your growing body in healthy and fun ways. We hope these spark you to learn more about how to choose foods that nourish both your body and your soul.

FUN FACT:

On average, Americans combined eat a total of about 100 acres of pizza a day or about 350 slices per second.

- **Be adventurous with new foods.** If there are foods you didn't like as a young child, give them a new try because your taste buds change in puberty too. And sometimes it just takes trying a new food a bunch of times before you start to like it. So keep trying new foods, and you might just discover some new favorites! Eating a variety of foods is the best way to give your body all the nutrients it needs to fight off illness and stay healthy.
- **Don't skip breakfast.** Eating breakfast wakes up your brain every morning and truly helps you think better in school! It's like starting your engine. Just make sure your breakfast isn't all sugar or sweets. You need protein to help your energy last and keep you feeling full. Breakfast doesn't have to be traditional breakfast foods; it can be any healthy option. Have you ever had a peanut butter and jelly sandwich for breakfast?
- **Eat small snacks between meals.** For an extra boost of energy for your body and brain, eat small snacks between your main meals. Foods like almonds or other nuts, cheese, an apple with peanut butter, yogurt or granola, or even an occasional cookie with a glass of milk are all good ways to get that boost.

■ **Eat 5 colorful fruits and vegetables every day.** The most colorful fruits and veggies provide important vitamins and minerals to help you grow taller and stronger and provide fiber, which helps you feel full longer. Try to eat 1 red, 1 orange or yellow, and 2 green fruits or veggies every day. Those make 4 servings, so for your fifth, you choose the color! Just remember that the color needs to be natural. Colored candies don't count!

■ **Eat more brown.** Even though we recommend eating lots of colors, we also recommend switching out white foods for brown foods. Brown foods have more fiber and carbs that are more useful to your body for energy. The fiber also helps you feel full (so you don't feel as grumpy or angry because you're hungry—or "hangry"). Fiber also acts as a "scrub brush" as it passes through your digestive system, helping keep it clean. Examples of white foods are pasta, white rice, white bread, and potatoes. To trade them for the healthier brown options, choose whole-grain pastas, brown rice, whole-grain breads, and sweet potatoes, which are technically orange!

■ **Drink water.** Your body needs 6 to 8 cups of water every day. That's because your body is mostly made of water! If you are active, you should drink even more water to make up for the sweat you lose. Water is definitely the best drink for almost every occasion. Drinking plenty of water helps keep your skin clear, your body healthy, and your brain working better. If water seems unsatisfying, you can add a slice of fruit or cucumber, or you can add a little fruit juice to give it a fresh flavor.

FUN FACT:
Did you know that 60% of your body is water? The brain and heart are 73% water, and the lungs are about 83% water. The skin contains 64% water; the muscles and kidneys, 79%. Even the bones are 31% water.

■ **Look for calcium.** Your bones can't grow without calcium (a mineral), and during puberty, you need more calcium than at any other time in your life. Calcium is in a lot of foods you probably eat regularly, but during puberty, you need 4 to 5 servings of calcium-rich foods every day, like dairy products (like milk, cheese, yogurt, or ice cream); soy products; calcium-fortified juices; or dark leafy green vegetables.

- ■ **Pack in some protein.** Try to eat 2 to 3 servings of protein a day. The best protein for growing comes from beans, nuts, peanut butter, low-fat dairy products, tofu, soy milk, or lean meats (like chicken, fish, or lean cuts of pork and beef). Protein is the major building block that helps keep your muscles strong and in good shape. Like fiber, protein helps you feel full longer, so you don't get *hangry.*

- ■ **Enjoy some sweets.** Is it OK to eat cookies? Fast food? Donuts? Soda pop? As long as they're not the only things you eat and they're not a daily habit, then yes, it's OK. Sweets are nice because they can be good for the soul, right? Just remember that foods with a lot of sugar or salt don't usually have as much of the important nutrients your growing body needs, so you need to make sure you eat plenty of other nutritious foods.

- ■ **Get busy in the kitchen!** Have fun learning how to prepare foods and dishes with your family. When you learn to cook or prepare foods, it helps you learn more about what you like. Maybe you can even plan a meal or two for your family each week! That's a great way to try new foods.

Move Your Body

It's no surprise that your body needs to move to stay healthy. Exercise is just that: moving your body. Exercise is important because it helps you keep your muscles working well, builds stronger bones, and keeps you more flexible and less likely to be injured. Did you know that exercise also keeps your brain happier and boosts your mood?

You should do your best to get a total of 60 minutes of movement every day. It doesn't have to be all at once, but it can add up throughout the day. For example, one day you might spend 10 minutes dancing, 30 minutes shooting hoops, 15 minutes walking the dog, and 10 minutes vacuuming the house.

Those add up to more than 60 minutes (and will probably make your dog and your parents very happy!).

People who exercise have lower risk for being overweight or having heart disease, diabetes, or other medical conditions later in life. Even though some people who are very healthy can develop these conditions because of their genes, these problems often develop from unhealthy habits.

The most important thing to remember when it comes to exercise is to keep it fun so you look forward to it every day. You don't have to run around a track, run on a treadmill, or go to an exercise class at the gym to get exercise. Instead, move your body in ways that make you happy! You can dance, play tag, ride your bike, skateboard, roller-skate, go on a hike, race your dog, or climb a tree. There are tons of ways to have fun and exercise at the same time.

Rest Your Body

Sleep is magical—truly. When you sleep, your body is doing amazing things. Most of your growth happens when you sleep. Your brain organizes your memories and everything you've learned. Your body repairs injuries or looks for ways to boost your health. Your dreams help you manage some of the big feelings you experience.

Because there's a lot of growing, strengthening, feeling, and learning that happens during puberty, sleep is especially important for you right now. If you are 8 to 10 years old, you need at least 9 to 12 hours every night. If you are 11 to 13, you need 9 to 10 hours. Even teenagers need at least 8 hours of sleep every night.

It is absolutely true that enough sleep . . .

- Gives you more energy
- Makes you happier and less moody
- Improves your memory and how well you focus
- Helps regulate your appetite and keep your weight healthier
- Fights off illness and infection

- Allows your muscles to grow stronger and more coordinated
- Protects your heart

The best way to help your body benefit from snoozing is to keep your sleep routine the same as often as you can. Try to be consistent with bedtimes and wake-up times every day, including weekends. Sure, staying up late sometimes or sleeping in sometimes is nice, but it can confuse your body and make you feel extra tired for a few days. A short nap can help make up for lost sleep, but longer naps can actually make it more difficult to fall and stay asleep. If you do experience trouble, your doctor can recommend some tips for better sleep.

FUN FACT:

You can survive without eating for several weeks, but you can survive about only 11 days with no sleep. The longest recorded time without sleep is about 264 hours, or just over 11 consecutive days.

Appreciate Your Body

If you are excited with these body changes, great! Enjoy them while they are happening. But if all this growing and changing leaves you feeling confused or downright unhappy with the way your body looks, that's OK too. What's most important to remember is that your body will continue to change. Most of these changes will help you accomplish amazing things, but you have to continue to take care of your body with healthy foods, movement, and rest.

The coolest thing about growing and about this time of your life is that you are not a little kid anymore. You are becoming stronger, smarter, and better at complicated stuff. You're gaining a lot of new skills and becoming more responsible. Look around. There are some kids your age who can do backflips, score soccer goals, write a song, run a 10K race, jump a horse, paint a landscape, do a double axel, climb a mountain, or skate a half-pipe. If you treat your body well and appreciate all it can do for you, you may be surprised by how awesome it can be!

Before you know it, you are growing, growing, GROWN!

CHAPTER 14

YOU'VE GOT THIS!

S tudents cheer as their buses pull into the entrance for Wonder World Amusement Park. It's the last day of school before summer break, and everyone is excited for the Bright Springs School End-of-Year Field Trip. It's the perfect sunny day for the students to celebrate the start of summer with their friends.

Jack sits in the back of the bus, relieved that it finally smells better after Mr Bellows stressed the importance of everyone showering often and using deodorant. Since it's going to be a long hot day, Jack is wearing his favorite type of deodorant and even has some in his backpack to reapply if he needs it. He's wearing a new T-shirt from his favorite band, and he doesn't want to get sweat stains on the bright pink fabric.

Maria got a buzz cut for the summer and loved the way it kept her cool when her team won their soccer game last week. Now she sits on the bus next to Quinn, a new friend she made when Quinn started their period last week. Maria shared a pad with Quinn, just like Shreya had done for Maria when she started her period for the first time. Quinn plays soccer too, and they spend the whole bus ride talking about their favorite athletes. So many of their role models also have periods, and that never seems to slow them down!

When the students leave the bus and head into the park, Oliver takes a long drink from his water bottle, making sure to stay hydrated in the hot sun. He also has a banana and some nuts in his backpack so he can fuel his body well to have the best day possible. Nancy walks with him, drinking from her own water bottle as she challenges Oliver to see who can win the biggest prize at the basketball toss game.

Stephanie tries out a few different rides before going to the Spinning Tops with Damien, whose glittery makeup sparkles in the sun. He showed her how to apply mascara this morning, but that's all the makeup she wants to wear for now. When the ride starts and they start spinning in circles, Stephanie throws her arms up into the air. She hasn't shaved her armpits in a few days, and she feels perfectly fine being a little hairy! Plus, underneath her black T-shirt, where no one can see, she's wearing a new bright pink bra that makes her chest feel perfectly supported.

Leshaun and Antonio are finally tall enough to ride the Green Dragon roller coaster. Antonio's newly colored purple hair blows around in the wind, and Leshaun throws his hands up and lets out a high-pitched scream as they fly down the biggest hill. Under his tie-dyed shorts, Leshaun is wearing new underwear that his dad recommended, which makes him feel covered and comfortable. When he gets off the ride, his only worry about standing up in front of his friends is how quickly he can get back in line for another turn.

When everyone heads to the Snack Shack for lunch, Kimi gives in to Jazmin begging and finally tries pineapple on pizza for the first time. After a few bites, she has to admit: it's pretty good after all. Jazmin claps and jumps up and down, with her long hair bouncing, and Shreya joins to try some too. When Jazmin spills pizza sauce on her new camo pants, Shreya shows her how to clean it up so it blends right in with the pattern.

When it's time to leave, the kids all head to the parking lot together, exhausted after a day of fun. They are about to climb back onto the buses when Kimi points toward a nearby car, calling out: "Look! It's Dr Wilson!"

All the students turn, waving to their guest from Guest Speaker Day, way back at the beginning of the year. Dr Wilson waves as she recognizes the students.

"Hey!" calls Maria.

"Thanks for teaching us about puberty!" Oliver calls.

"It helped us a lot!" Jack says.

"We learned so much this year!" Jack yells.

"Do we look older?" Stephanie asks.

Dr Wilson smiles at all the kids.

"You look like you're all doing great," says Dr Wilson. "You got this! Keep being you!"

Now that you're almost through *You-ology*, we hope you understand a lot more about puberty and what's ahead. You've got this, right? Sometimes you'll feel like you do, but if you don't always feel like that, it's not only OK but also totally normal. With so much going on, it takes time to adjust to the changes and grow your confidence. As silly as it may sound, it takes time for you to understand YOU.

WHO ARE YOU?

Deep in your brain, there's a question you'll probably start to wonder about. Thinking about this question a lot is common for kids as they become preteens, teens, and even young adults. And although it sounds like a super simple question, the answer is complicated and may not always be the same.

Here's the question: *Who are you?*

There are a million ways to answer that question. You can keep it simple by saying just your name, but there's a lot more to you than just your name.

You have likes, dislikes, dreams, fears, difficulties, and talents—and you are a unique combination of ALL these things. There's no way you could tell someone all the unique things that make you, *you*! That makes answering that question really hard.

Have you ever heard the saying *"actions speak louder than words"*? That means that what you do or don't do tells others a lot about who you are. You may do some things on purpose to let others know more about you. An example would be wearing your favorite team's jersey to show you are a fan. Other times, you may not even think about what you are doing or not doing; you're just doing what comes naturally, what feels enjoyable, or what feels right. That's when you are just "being you."

I LIKE YOUR STYLE!

As kids go through puberty, many become more interested in expressing themselves through things like clothing, hair, and accessories; hats, jewelry, or even buttons on their backpacks; or stickers on their lockers. These are fun ways to show others more about yourself and what you like.

As we covered in Chapter 3, when it comes to your personal style, the way you choose to look to others is called your *gender expression*. You may not even think you have a "style" yet, but you do.

Once you begin dressing yourself and having opinions about what you like or don't like, you are developing your gender expression, which includes the clothing you wear, how you cut or style your hair, and how you "decorate" yourself with things like jewelry, hats, shoes, or makeup. Some kids like to wear dresses or jewelry and to paint their nails. Some kids like to wear camo, hats, and boots. Some kids like to wear athletic shirts or sweatpants and to keep their hair short. Some might even like to switch their style up with a football jersey and a frilly skirt. The options are endless, and many kids switch it up a lot—it's all about what feels best.

There is no right or wrong way to express yourself. And remember, you can't know someone's gender identity by the way they look. You can't know how they feel on the inside by looking at their gender expression on the outside.

Just like it's important for you to express yourself in the ways that feel best for you, all kids should do the same. Everyone deserves to feel comfortable with being themself instead of feeling like they need to look or act a certain way because of their gender or what others expect.

YOU DO YOU

Just like certain clothes aren't just for boys or just for girls, what you like to do and how you are supposed to act aren't determined by whether you are a boy or a girl. Remember, when people think that every person or thing belongs to the same category, it's called a **stereotype.** So a **gender stereotype** is when someone believes *all* girls should have longer hair, wear dresses, enjoy getting their nails done, and be best friends with other girls. Common stereotypes for boys include believing that *all* boys should have short hair; enjoy sports, cars, and dinosaurs; and hang out only with other boys.

Can a girl have a best friend who is a boy? Can a boy paint his fingernails? Can anyone play football? Can a boy have a crush on a boy? If you answered yes to all these questions, you're correct! Your gender doesn't determine how you act, whom you like, what you enjoy doing, or even what you wear. YOU determine that!

During puberty, it's really common for kids to try new things. Because this is a time when it's normal to wonder, "Who am I?" you may want to try out new looks, new styles, new interests, new friends, and even new personalities. That's totally OK. Some will feel right, and some won't. That's how you learn and become more comfortable with who you are and how you like to express yourself. That's how *you do you!*

THEY DO THEM

Just like you want other kids to respect you for who you are, they deserve the same respect. You don't want others to think they know everything about you by the way you dress or act, so remember that you can't know much about anyone else by just their gender expression.

Let's think about some of the characters in this book. In the stories, you learned some things about them but *not* everything. Here's a little more about each of them.

Shreya is on a swim team and is the fastest in backstroke. She was born with a hearing difficulty and depends on hearing aids, but nobody can hear underwater, so that's one of the reasons she grew to love swimming. Her favorite class is art because she loves drawing mandalas and telling her friends about her favorite festival, Holi, which is messier than her art class! Her grandparents recently moved in with her family, and her grandmother is teaching her how to cook.

Jazmin has 2 sisters and 3 brothers, 2 dads, a mom, and 3 cats. She loves to tap-dance and play basketball with her best friend, Oliver. She also enjoys baking sweets, especially decorating sugar cookies. Jazmin has superpowers in geography; she knows the capital of every country in the world!

Damien is the tallest boy in his class and likes to experiment with makeup on himself or his friends. His favorite class is science, and he wants to be a chemistry teacher. Recently, he's become more interested in his art class because he gets to sit next to his crush, Shreya.

Quinn is shy and quiet, but at the skateboard park, everybody knows them because Quinn can do amazing ollies and other tricks. At home, Quinn likes to sew and make their own clothes. At school, Quinn feels uncomfortable when a teacher tries to divide the class into boy and girl groups because Quinn is nonbinary and they don't feel like they fit into either group. Quinn's friends have helped teachers find other ways to group students.

Nancy is Native American and a member of the Cherokee Nation. She loves listening to her grandmother talk about their heritage, and she especially enjoys taking dance classes at her tribal center. Her hobbies are reading, playing the trumpet, and sewing. She is learning to sew as her grandmother helps her work on her regalia. Her closet is full of pink and flowered, ruffled clothes, as well as a collection of tiny vests she made for her pet guinea pig. She's also really good at basketball even though she doesn't play very often.

Antonio is Latino and speaks Spanish at home with his family. He spends most of his time in sports. His favorites are soccer, swimming, and

Damien Nancy Jazmin Shreya Quinn Antonio

rock climbing. He has an aunt who is a firefighter, and that's what he wants to be when he grows up. He not only is all about safety but also loves to prank his friends. He has a dog named Ketchup.

All the characters are just as interesting as each other, and each one has a unique story, just like you and every one of your friends. Like you and like them, EVERY body is changing and every person is learning more about themself as they grow up. None of them fits into any one stereotype because of their gender identity or their sex assigned at birth. Neither do you nor your friends. That is what makes people so interesting and unique!

If you have classmates or friends who are expressing themselves in new ways, they're doing exactly what they are supposed to be doing—figuring out who they are. You can support them by accepting them no matter how they choose to express themselves. Remember the Golden Rule from Chapter 2, and treat them with respect. It's not OK to gossip about them. It's also not OK to ignore them completely. You wouldn't want others to treat you that way. You can always be respectful and kind. You do you! They do them!

THE END AND A NEW BEGINNING

Although you've reached the end of this book, it may be just the beginning of puberty for you. And even if you're already midway through puberty, you will still do a lot more growing, in your body and mind, for years to come. Now that you've learned about all the things that happen, you don't have to wonder or worry whether you're ever going to look older. You know you will.

Reading a book like this also helps you realize that the word *puberty* doesn't need to make you feel awkward. You know it's not just about pubic hair, periods, and voice "cracks." It's about bigger and more important stuff than those.

So yes, you will get a new "look," and your body will do new things, but you will also become more mature. You will make new friends, and you'll learn to be a better friend. You'll have new skills, new smarts, and new feelings too. Those are the things that will help you build your confidence and turn you into the very best version of you!

We hope you feel more prepared for the things that may be happening now or soon. And even though this book is to help YOU understand YOUR changes, we hope it has helped you understand what your friends and classmates may be experiencing too.

Remember that even though EVERY body goes through puberty, your journey will be unique to you, and other kids' journeys will be unique to them. That uniqueness keeps the world (and your friends) a lot more interesting!

You've got this! Keep being YOU!

GLOSSARY

Throughout this book, there are lots of words describing bodies, products, and other important topics that are related to puberty. You will find all the words explained in more detail in the book, but we thought it would be helpful to have them right here too!

acne—when someone has blackheads and pimples on their skin, sometimes called *zits*

anus—the opening where your bowel movements (poop) exit your body

apocrine glands—a type of sweat gland in your armpits, feet, palms, and groin; beginning in puberty, these glands release an oily yellowish substance along with sweat

areola—the circle of darker skin that surrounds the nipples on the chest

athletic cup—a smooth curved piece of hard plastic that protects the penis and testes from injury

bigender—a gender identity used to describe someone who feels like both a boy and a girl

binary—something made up of only 2 parts

binding—wearing binders, or special types of tank tops, that compress the breasts to make them less noticeable through clothing

biological parents—the 2 people who supplied the sperm and the egg to make a baby

breast bud—a small hard knot under the areola and nipple that signals the start of breast development

bystanders—people watching a situation occur but not directly involved

cervix—an opening that connects the uterus and vagina

cesarean delivery/C-section—when a baby is delivered by a surgery instead of through the vagina

circumcision—a minor surgery to remove the foreskin from the tip of the penis

cisgender—a gender identity used to describe someone whose sex assigned at birth is the same as the gender they feel on the inside; *cis-* means "same"

cleavage—the crease line formed between breasts when they meet in the middle, usually because they are pushed together by a bra or clothing

clique—a group of friends that either can be welcoming to people or can exclude others

clitoris—the part of the vulva that is very sensitive to touch; the bump at the top of the labia minora is the tip of the clitoris, and the rest is inside the body

contractions—when the uterus squeezes and relaxes during labor to help push a baby out

cramps/menstrual cramps—cramping of the uterus that is felt in the lower abdomen or pelvis often before or during periods

cyberbullying—when hurtful comments or untrue messages about a person are posted online; it can also occur through text messages, direct messages, or pictures of someone that are posted without their permission

cycle length—the number of days from the first day of one period to the first day of the next

eccrine sweat glands—a type of sweat gland that pushes out mostly water to cool the body

egg—a type of cell in the ovaries that is required to make a baby

ejaculation—when semen is released from the urethra during an erection

endometrium—the inner layer of the uterus that is released with a period

epididymis—a small and tightly coiled tube where sperm finish growing

erection—when the penis becomes firm or hard and sticks up

estrogen—a hormone made mostly in the ovaries

fallopian tubes—the 2 armlike tubes at the top of the uterus that allow the egg to travel from the ovary to the uterus

feminine—a type of gender expression (like clothing, appearance, or behaviors) that society links with girls, although it can actually be for anyone

foreskin—a rim of skin that covers the glans (head) of a penis

gender binary—the assumption that there are only 2 genders: girl or boy (woman or man)

gender diverse—a term that includes all gender identities except cisgender

gender dysphoria—the distress someone may feel when their physical body is different from that of their gender identity

gender expression—the way someone expresses themself on the outside through characteristics like clothing, hairstyle, or behaviors

gender fluid—a gender identity when someone's inner sense of gender changes from time to time

gender identity—knowing and feeling that you're a boy, a girl, both, or neither (no matter what genitals you have)

gender stereotype—the incorrect assumption that someone should act a certain way and like certain things because of the sex they were assigned at birth

genetics—the traits and physical features you inherit through your biological parents

genitalia/genitals—body parts between the legs, including either a vulva or a penis and scrotum

glans—the tip of the penis (also called the *head*)

Golden Rule—a lesson that appears in most cultures to encourage people to treat others the way they want to be treated

groin—the area around your genitals where your upper thighs meet your body

growth hormone—a hormone that increases a lot during puberty to help you grow taller

gynecomastia—a small amount of breast growth in bodies with mainly testosterone

hormones—chemical messengers from your brain that tell your body parts important things, like when to begin puberty

intersex—a sex other than male or female that is used when someone's body (inside or outside parts) doesn't fit into the typical male category or female category

inverted nipple—a nipple that pulls inward instead of poking out or lying flat

labia majora—the thicker, outer lips of the vulva

labia minora—the thinner, inner lips of the vulva

labor—the process of giving birth

larynx—the voice box; the bump in the neck around the larynx is sometimes referred to as an "Adam's apple"

masculine—a type of gender expression (like clothing, appearance, or behaviors) that society links with boys, although it can actually be for anyone

masturbation—when someone is touching their own genitals in a way that feels good

menarche—the very first period, or menstrual flow, during puberty

menstrual cycle—the ongoing changes in hormones and the endometrium that prepare the body for pregnancy; if pregnancy does not occur, a menstrual period begins

menstruation/menstrual flow/menstrual period—the time when bloody fluid comes out of the vagina, typically lasting about 3 to 7 days; it is also known as a period

modest—a description of someone who wants privacy when dressing and undressing or who wants to keep their naked body private

mons—the fatty soft area over the pubic bone where pubic hair grows

nipple—the hard little bump inside the circle of darker skin on the chest

nocturnal emission—when someone ejaculates while sleeping; it is also referred to as a *wet dream*

nonbinary—a gender identity for someone who doesn't feel like either a girl or a boy on the inside, or they may feel like some of both

nutrients—the smaller parts of your food that are absorbed and used by your body after you digest what you eat

orgasm—the intense good feeling that can occur with masturbation and other times when someone's genitals are made to feel good

ovary—an internal body part that contains egg cells and releases estrogen; it is located next to the uterus and near the end of each fallopian tube and is about the size of a walnut

pad/sanitary napkin—an oval or rectangular cottony piece of material that is placed in underwear to absorb menstrual blood; it is a type of period product

panty liner—a small pad sometimes worn in underwear to absorb vaginal discharge or light menstrual flow

penis—a body part where urine (pee) comes out; it hangs down in front of the body

period—the time when bloody fluid slowly flows out of the vagina, typically for 3 to 7 days; it is also known as menstruation

period products—pads, tampons, menstrual cups, and period underwear that help manage periods

pituitary gland—a tiny, pea-sized gland in the brain that releases many different hormones, including the ones that start puberty

PMS (premenstrual syndrome)—a variety of physical and emotional changes experienced by some people before a period starts

pornography (porn)—photos or videos of naked people (usually actors) doing private things with their bodies that differs from what most people do with their naked bodies

precocious puberty—puberty that starts earlier than what's considered normal

prostate gland—an inside body part that adds fluid to sperm to make semen

puberty—the time (years) when a body changes from being childlike to being more adultlike

pubic hair—the hair that grows around the genitals

scrotum—a pouch of thin skin that holds the 2 testes

semen—a liquid that is made of sperm plus fluids from the prostate gland and seminal vesicles

seminal vesicles—an inside body part that adds fluid to sperm to make semen

sex assigned at birth—the sex assigned to a baby when they are born; it is usually based on their genitals and can be male, female, or intersex

sexual abuse—wrong and harmful interaction when someone looks at or touches a child's genitals, has a child look at or touch theirs, or even shows them pictures or videos of naked bodies

shaft—the longer part of the penis that is attached to the body

sperm—a type of cell made in the testes that is required to make a baby

spontaneous erection—an erection that occurs at random times for no obvious reason

stereotype—the incorrect assumption that ALL people in a certain category are the same

stretch marks—groups of purple to red lines that sometimes show up on skin during times of fast growth

supernumerary nipple—an extra nipple

tampon—a small cylinder-shaped period product that fits inside the vagina to absorb menstrual blood

testes/testicles—2 round body parts that are held behind the penis, in the scrotum, and make testosterone and sperm

testosterone—a hormone made by the testes that helps start puberty for children and teens with testes

toxic shock syndrome (TSS)—a very rare but serious bacterial infection that has been linked to incorrect tampon use

transgender—a gender identity used to describe someone whose sex assigned at birth is different from their gender identity; *trans-* means "cross" or "opposite"

tucking—when someone tucks their penis and scrotum back between their legs to make the bump less noticeable

urethra—the opening where urine (pee) comes out, located either just below the clitoris or at the tip of the penis

uterus—the inside body part where babies grow and where a period comes from

vagina—a tunnel-like body part that connects the uterus to the outside through an opening on the vulva (see *vulva* below). It is where periods and most babies leave the body.

vaginal discharge—creamy white or yellowish fluid that normally comes out of the vagina

vas deferens—a long tube that connects the testes to the penis, allowing sperm and semen to leave the body

vulva—the area between the legs that includes the labia majora, labia minora, clitoris, opening to the urethra, and opening to the vagina

wet dream—ejaculation that happens during sleep

ACKNOWLEDGMENTS

Writing a book is always an adventure in curating our knowledge and experiences from the past, writing in the moment, and keeping an eye to the future. We feel like we've succeeded, but it wasn't just the 3 of us. As usual, we'd like to thank our village, starting with the American Academy of Pediatrics (AAP) Publishing team for inviting us to create what kids have deserved for a long time—one puberty book for EVERY body.

This book wouldn't be in your hands without Barrett Winston, senior manager of publishing acquisitions at the AAP. Barrett saw the need for a puberty book that lets EVERY child feel seen. She had the courage, passion, and perseverance to make this happen, despite it being the first consumer book the AAP has published for youth. Barrett also had the vision to bring together the Girlology cofounders and a pediatrician with expertise in inclusive health education for all kids.

We are also grateful to our amazing editor and new BFF, Kathryn Sparks, for keeping us on schedule and for fiercely protecting (and appropriately editing) our voice in keeping this book educational but fun. A big thank-you also goes to Sara Hoerdeman, marketing manager, who was incredibly patient as we noodled and re-noodled titles, cover ideas, and every possible way we could get this book into the hands of young people. And we are greatly appreciative of Jeff Mahony and Shannan Martin with the AAP Publishing team, who were also instrumental in making this project become a reality.

Facts are cool, but stories really help children relate to a book about puberty, so we are especially thankful for the talent of Laura Essex, who wrote the stories that begin each chapter. We are amazed by her ability to capture common experiences of kids navigating puberty in such a fun, colorful, and approachable way.

Then, our stories and facts were brought to life by our favorite illustrator, Lisa Perrett, who has illustrated other books by the Girlology team. The day we received Lisa's illustrations of the characters in this book was one of the most fun days of this whole project. It was truly a gift to see her artistic representations of our diverse characters and her kid-friendly illustrations that make puberty facts easier to understand and remember.

Our heartfelt appreciation also goes to the AAP groups that graciously and carefully reviewed this book and provided invaluable feedback. Specifically, we'd like to thank the Section on Lesbian, Gay, Bisexual, and Transgender Health and Wellness, the Section on Developmental and Behavioral Pediatrics, and the Task Force on Mental Health. We are humbled by your expertise in each of these areas and are grateful to have had your input in order to make this book the best it can be. Beyond the AAP Publishing team and advisory groups, we want to thank the AAP as a whole for being our nation's leader in child advocacy and working tirelessly to help all kids thrive.

We also acknowledge Girlology/Guyology for providing the foundation for our content, and from that team, we are grateful to Jonathan Long and Katrina Graczyk for their generosity in sharing ideas and supporting us in taking the time away from our "real jobs" to write.

The feedback from multiple families that reviewed this book was truly priceless. To Henry Keefer, Tom Rose, Sage Rose, Paxton McCausland, Kassia Finn, and Tonya Shonkwiler, as well as those who prefer to not have their names listed, we hope you know that your feedback helped make this book truly speak to EVERY body.

To all the young people we have had the privilege to care for and teach, and to the gender-diverse kids who have had the courage to ask for a puberty book that includes EVERY body, we have heard you, and we thank you for your voice and all you have taught us. From the bottom of our hearts, we hope this book meets your expectations and helps us all get one step closer to living in a world where every person is seen, valued, and respected.

Most of all, we thank our spouses and our kids, who supported us in taking on this project—during a pandemic nonetheless. From helping us come up with fun facts, to voting on titles, to giving us lots of feedback, you have made us forever grateful. Your love, support, guidance, and tolerance mean the world to us. We are so happy that you're proud of us, even though we love talking about puberty!

INDEX